"James Robertson is the most experienced expert i
ever more urgent in the continuing financial debac
Future Money is his magnum opus, synthesizing his key insights from 30 years of practice and scholarly activism illuminating the role of money in human societies and the secretive politics of money-creation. Robertson's proposals for reform from global to local are still the most realistic and achievable. Newly energized and activated by the worldwide Occupy movements of aware citizens representing 99% of humanity, Robertson's sane, humane, ecological monetary systems are at last, flourishing worldwide in many towns, and his lifelong ethical, tenacious crusading is bearing fruit." – Hazel Henderson, author of *Ethical Markets: Growing the Green Economy* and President of Ethical Markets Media (USA and Brazil)

"If a Martian landed and said take me to your future leader, how much happier we would be if we could lead them to the door of James Robertson. He is the great, creative economic thinker of recent times. *Future Money* explores how better systems of value and exchange could set us all free." – Ed Mayo, Secretary General, Co-operatives UK

"The shape of the future depends on whether – and how quickly – the world wakes up and realises that the economy must work within ecological limits. *Future Money* explains why this is the case and is a call to each and every one of us to challenge prevailing assumptions about the economy, as well as to contribute to a different way of thinking and acting. Recommended reading if you think the economy exists in order to benefit people and planet rather than just a tool for the rich to get richer." – Caroline Lucas, MP

"People still ignore the chronic dysfunctionalities at the heart of our money system, and refuse to acknowledge how big a part that 'failed system' plays in our current economic crisis. *Future Money* lays bare those dysfunctionalities with forensic skill, unhesitatingly 'naming names' as to who is responsible, and then lays out a programme of radical reform for our money system that is utterly compelling. I can guarantee it will change the way people think about today's crisis – and, hopefully, the way they act." – Jonathon Porritt, Founder, Forum for the Future

"James Robertson in lucid and clear arguments exposes the unsound system on which money rests. Through his deep analysis of today's financial crisis, Robertson's *Future Money* gives an honest and convincing look at how today's money system has to change now, before it is too late. An important resource for all of us concerned to act to ensure our collective future." – Wendy Harcourt, Editor, *Development*, International Institute of Social Studies, Erasmus University, The Hague

"James Robertson is an man of extraordinary experience and eminence. If we are looking for somebody to provide the world with the model it needs to save us from economic anarchy he is an ideal candidate. Unlike the critiques that have been published in their thousands by people who before 2008 had barely thought about what money is, this is a book of depth by a man who has been developing sane and equitable solutions for the past 40 years. He provides practical answers to the management of money systems at local, national and global levels. Every civil servant in the Treasury should be forced to read this book." – Molly Scott Cato, Reader in Green Economics at the University of Wales Institute, Cardiff (UWIC) and Director of Cardiff Institute for Co-operative Studies

"James Robertson has provided clear, convincing and practical proposals for comprehensive modernisation of world monetary systems, a subject on which he has been a leading thinker for four decades. Given the current financial crisis the time has come for economic and political leaders to pay close attention to his wise counsel." – Mary Mellor, author of *The Future of Money: from financial crisis to public resource*

"Money is a manmade device which dominates our lives. Yet few people really understand how the monetary system actually works. James Robertson has a clear grasp of this complex subject, which makes his latest book, *Future Money*, both fascinating to read and vitally important in helping us to understand the radical reforms which are urgently required. His explanation of how money is created and how governments collect and spend it will be a revelation to most people – even to many bankers! By reminding us that money is our servant, this book shows how money can be used as the means by which we can create a new economic system that is both just and sustainable. This is a book that has to be read not just by politicians and bankers, but by every citizen who wants to escape the tyranny of money and the austerity regimes that it is currently imposing on us." – James Skinner, Trustee, Organic Research Centre and Trustee Emeritus, the new economics foundation

FUTURE MONEY

BREAKDOWN OR BREAKTHROUGH?

JAMES ROBERTSON

green books

For Alison, without whom this
book could not have been written.

Words of wisdom

"It will often be to no purpose to tell of the superior advantages the subjects of a well-governed state enjoy; that they are better lodged, better clothed, better fed. These considerations will commonly make no great impression. You will be more likely to persuade, if you describe the great system of public policy which procures these advantages; if you explain the connexions and dependencies of its several parts, their mutual subordination to one another, and their general subserviency to the happiness of society; if you show how this system might be introduced . . ., what it is that hinders it from taking place at present, how those obstructions might be removed, and all the several wheels of the machine of government be made to move with more harmony and smoothness, without grating upon one another, or mutually retarding one another's motions. It is scarce possible that a man should listen to a discourse of this kind, and not feel himself animated to some degree of public spirit. He will, at least for the moment, feel some desire to remove those obstructions and to put into motion so beautiful and so orderly a machine." (Adam Smith, *The Theory of Moral Sentiments*, Part IV, Chapter II, pp. 217-218, Cambridge Texts in the History of Philosophy).

"O wad some Power the giftie gie us
To see oursels as ithers see us!" (Robert Burns)

"The toad beneath the harrow knows / Exactly where each tooth-point goes. The butterfly upon the road / Preaches contentment to that toad."
(Rudyard Kipling, "Pagett M.P.", 1886)

"Lord, what fools these mortals be!" (Shakespeare, *A Midsummer Night's Dream*)

"Uncontrollable laughter arose among the blessed gods." (Homer, *The Odyssey*)

"*Beyond* laughter? . . . The Greek gods were once passionately involved in the affairs of men. Then they confined themselves to looking down from Olympus and laughing. And for ages now they have been asleep." (Milan Kundera, *The Book of Laughter and Forgetting*, p.217, Penguin, 1983)

"The threatened collapse of our Western civilization has nothing to do with the political issues between capitalism and communism, but is the consequence of its false money system." (Frederick Soddy, 1877-1956, Nobel Prize in Chemistry 1921 and author of *Wealth, Virtual Wealth and Debt: The Solution to the Economic Paradox*, 1926. For reference see http://tinyurl.com/6v8lbb4)

"He either fears his fate too much or his deserts are small, who dares not put it to the touch to win or lose it all." (Earl of Montrose, 1640s)

First published in the UK in 2012
by Green Books Ltd,
Dartington Space, Dartington Hall,
Totnes, Devon TQ9 6EN

Print edition ISBN 978 1 900322 98 0
PDF format ISBN 978 0 85784 084 4
ePub format ISBN 978 0 85784 085 1

Printed by TJ International, Padstow, Cornwall, UK

Contents

Preface

I am finishing writing this book in January 2012. As the prospects for the eurozone and the rest of our global money system worsen day by day, it becomes clearer and clearer that our national and international leaders and their professional financial advisers will not be able to clear up the mess they have left us in. The voices of protest are now rising in the streets.

The need for a comprehensive modernisation of the world's money system is becoming more and more urgent. It must be put in hand immediately. It must not be put off until quieter times. Indeed, quieter times will not come until it has been carried out.

Will we decide to put this modernisation in hand without delay in response to the present emergency? The answer will almost certainly help to determine how much longer human civilisation will survive and evolve in anything like its present form. As I suggest in this book, radical reform of the money system will be a necessary condition, though perhaps not by itself a sufficient condition, of the survival of anything like our present civilisation, and perhaps of our species, beyond the end of this century.

The fact is that today's professional understanding of how the money system works is still at a primitive stage. As we shall see, it parallels in significant ways the failure in pre-Copernican times to understand that the Earth goes round the sun, not vice versa.

The message of this book is that a Copernican revolution in human understanding of how the money system works and how it ought to work is more and more urgently overdue. In the case of the money system, unlike the solar system, this revolution will not only be intellectual and scientific. It will also be a revolution in practice. This understanding goes far beyond that of the present conventional experts in money – practitioners and academics alike. This new understanding can be summarised as follows.

Money is a system of quantitative values – distinct, numerical currency values. How it works motivates people to live in some ways instead of others. As long as we allow it to work as it now does, it will continue to conflict with real-life human values. How it now encourages or compels almost everyone in the world to live is inevitably leading us towards a combined collapse of the interacting systems – ecological, social and economic – on which we depend. That is why reforming it will be necessary for our survival, though perhaps not by itself a sufficient condition of it.[1]

Meanwhile, if unreformed, its workings will continue to frustrate all the well-meant efforts of active citizens, NGOs (non-governmental organisations) and government agencies, to deal with our present ills and problems – including worldwide poverty, environmental destruction, social injustice, economic inefficiency, and political unrest and violence within and between nations. Again, that is why failure to reform the world's money system urgently and radically – that is to say, from its roots up – could bring on the self-destruction of our civilisation before the end of this century.[2]

This book proposes a comprehensive set of reforms that would help to avoid that catastrophe. But, because established financial and economic thinking is so limited and out of date, most practising professional and academic experts in economics, finance and banking may dismiss the book's proposals as outside the boundaries of their concern. They include the politicians and government officials responsible for managing the money system. Even those few who see the need for the proposed reforms will find it impossible to put them into practice without strong support and pressure from outsiders, including active citizens and NGOs.

"By what authority are you saying these things to us, Mr Robertson?" That was what a middle-aged clergyman asked me, after a talk on the future of work in the 1970s at a conference at St George's House, Windsor Castle.[3] It has stuck in my mind ever since. People naturally want reassurance before committing serious time and effort to digesting new ideas.

Because I have no higher authority than my own to support the conclusions and proposals in this book, this Preface is largely about the personal background from which they have come. I hope it will help to show that those conclusions and proposals are worth taking seriously, as an outcome of common sense and years of independent study and exchange of views with other thoughtful and experienced people.

---

1. Another necessary condition will be a human population no larger than the world's resources can support. 2. For a fuller account of these two paragraphs, see the Introduction following this Preface. 3. This was one of the conferences organised by Professor Charles Handy, to whom I am still grateful for his support at that time.

My father's family background in Scotland and my mother's in Yorkshire, together with a Scottish and Yorkshire upbringing and schooling during the 1939-1945 war, gave me a fairly responsible, no-nonsense, rather conformist attitude to life – mildly prejudiced against London and the soft south-east of England.

Traditional university studies at Oxford – classics, history and philosophy (Mods and Greats, 1946-50) – helped to develop an interest in how changes take place in human affairs, and the root causes that make things happen. In retrospect, I am glad not to have had a formal education in economics and money and to have learned about them in practice later within a wider context of ideas.[4]

Working as a young Whitehall official in the Colonial Office in the 1950s involved me in the processes and progress of decolonisation. Helping to draw up early development plans for the islands of Mauritius and Seychelles led to an interest in finance and economics – and wakened doubts about the competence of the UK Treasury.

I visited those islands and other remaining British colonial territories with government ministers. On the most memorable of these trips I represented the Colonial Office on Prime Minister Harold Macmillan's 1960 tour of Africa, and introduced the theme of 'the wind of change is blowing through Africa' into drafts for his speeches.[5] After his speech in Cape Town, the tour became known as the 'Wind of Change' tour of Africa.

My selection for that assignment had been complicated by the fact that my father, Sir James Robertson, would be our host in Nigeria. He was the last British governor-general of that country, which became independent later in 1960. The question was whether having me on the PM's staff might cause awkwardness during our stay in Nigeria. It might have done, if any serious policy differences had arisen between the UK government and the governor-general there.[6] Luckily all concerned were satisfied that my father and I were both reliable enough to ensure that no difficulty would arise.

In those years I came to understand that deliberate, planned decolonisa-

---

4. A formal education in economics can badly limit people's perceptions of reality – confirming my long-time friend Hazel Henderson's well-known definition of "economics as a form of brain damage". However I do also understand that, in this day and age, learning that my proposals are based on the experiences of an elderly, white, Oxbridge male may automatically turn some readers off! 5. Colin Baker verifies this in *State of Emergency: Crisis in Central Africa, Nyasaland, 1959-1960*, Tauris, London, 1997: Chapter 6, 'The wind of change', pp 179-202. 6. As there were in Nyasaland (now Malawi) in our visit there later on the tour.

tion of power is a necessary counterpart to action for peaceful and constructive liberation, and that that is a principle widely relevant to the peaceful evolution of human life in society. It is a principle that has influenced much of my thinking since then. It needs to be more widely recognised and practised in public affairs – as well as in bringing up children – although in neither case can it always be straightforward.

I now see a parallel between the decolonisation of the European empires in Africa fifty years ago and what is happening to the world's money system today. Just as increasing numbers of African people experienced continuing rule by Europeans in the 1950s, so increasing numbers of people almost everywhere in the world are now experiencing the way money works as a dominating, exploitative, unjust, alien burden.

The wind of change is now blowing through the world's money system more and more strongly. As the majority of people, not responsible for the continuing world financial crisis that began in 2007/8, increasingly suffer injustice in paying off the banking and government debts incurred by 'I'm-alright-Jack' people richer than themselves, political pressure to be freed from that burden will continue to grow.[7]

Following that African tour, there came three years in the UK Cabinet Office working personally for Norman Brook, the then Secretary of the Cabinet, head of the Civil Service, and joint head of the Treasury – and, after him, for his successor Burke Trend. I respected and enjoyed working with both, and sympathised with Brook's private grumbles at being "on the wrong end of the bell" from ministers at the other end of it. My experience of the workings of government led to my first book, *The Reform of British Central Government*, published in 1971 after I had left the Civil Service.[8]

Meanwhile, my stint in the Cabinet Office had been followed by a move into the newly unified Ministry of Defence, to help to rationalise back-up services between Navy, Army and Royal Air Force. They ranged between such things as aircraft maintenance workshops, staff colleges, and the musical bands of the Navy, Army and RAF; the different ways the services codified the vast ranges of hardware they used; and much else. I found it enlightening and frustrating to work in a bloated organisation where many people's jobs seemed to be simply providing work for one another. But it gave me an interest in the new approaches of that time to management and organisation,

7. This is now already happening, supported by 'anti-capitalist' street protests. 8. For details of this and my other books, see www.jamesrobertson.com/books.htm.

systems analysis, computing, operational research and futures studies. In the mid-1960s I surprised my friends by leaving the Civil Service and joining a consultancy in 'management science'.

Not long after that, the big banks head-hunted me to set up IBRO (the Inter-Bank Research Organisation) to help them to develop electronic money transmission between each other's computers. By then I had become interested enough in how the money system worked to accept the banks' invitation. I spent nearly five years with them (1968-1973).

During that period, in addition to working for the banks, I was asked to give part-time advice to the House of Commons Procedure Committee on 'Scrutiny of Public Expenditure and Administration' (1968-69) and 'Scrutiny of Taxation' (1969-70) and to write memoranda for the Committee. I then led a team on 'The Future of London as an International Financial Centre', reporting to the Central Policy Review Staff in the Cabinet Office. My journey through the money system was getting under way.[9]

After the banks, in 1973 I became an independent writer, speaker and adviser on aspects of future economic, social and political change, working with Alison Pritchard who later became my wife.

That change of career freed me to catch up with a lot of what had been happening in the previous twenty years that I had not been following. I became interested in the environmental movement, the women's movement, futures studies, and the 'convivial society' ideas of Ivan Illich and the 'small-is-beautiful' thinking of E.F. (Fritz) Schumacher, both of whom it was a privilege to get to know personally.[10]

On the rebound after twenty years in the big systems of government, business and money,[11] my earlier involvement in decolonisation attracted me to the idea of people liberating ourselves from being too dependent on those big systems, and developing more local and personal ways of organising our

---

9. http://tinyurl.com/782nwu6. 10. It was an inspiring experience to attend the centenary celebrations, in October 2011 at Bristol, of E. F. Schumacher's birth. 11. Thirty years later I read James Lovelock's following comment to the *Financial Times*, 27 April 2007, about his scientific work: "There are very few scientists who have the chances I've had of working entirely independently, and not being constrained by the need to do work that will bring my next grant in. I would never have been allowed to develop Gaia at a university or a government department or an industrial one. You could only do it alone." That reflected my own gratitude for having been able to change to a more independent way of work in the 1970s; and it heightened my awareness of how much a society loses, when greater numbers of experienced and open-minded people do not see similar changes as possible for them.

lives – our work, food, technologies, health, education, money (local currencies and other local financial services), and so on.[12]

I still see this shift of emphasis towards local and personal co-operative self-reliance as a vitally necessary response to the future that human societies now face. But that does not mean we can just decide to detach ourselves en masse from the big interlocking systems of government, business and money. For one thing, in today's global village there are obviously crucial matters to be dealt with at national and international levels. For another, the people running those big systems won't easily let go of the power they have over us now. It is wishing for the moon to hope that they will voluntarily get off our backs without being encouraged or compelled to do so. Smooth and peaceful liberation will only be achieved when it is matched by deliberate, planned giving up of power – decolonisation.

That is why 'pre-political' action is needed to prepare the ground for deliberate, peaceful deep-seated changes in democratic societies. A climate of opinion must be created quickly that brings constructive proposals on to the political agenda. Otherwise, politicians and officials and other people making their upward career paths – including established commentators in the media – will be reluctant even to discuss those new alternatives, in case they risk possible harm to their careers by being seen as mavericks.[13]

Now, when the need for radical institutional change is urgent, the developing capacity of the internet to provide people-to-people instantaneous mass communication may quicken that pre-political process. But, in order to achieve practical progress, it will have to communicate a constructive agenda for the future, as well as encouraging demonstrations and protests against the present.

I came out with three new books in the 1970s. Two short ones, *Profit or People* (1974) and *Power, Money and Sex* (1976), were published by Marion Boyars in her Ideas in Progress series. They prepared the way for Alison and me to manage our own publication of *The Sane Alternative* (1978, second edition 1983). It was based on the twin concepts of 'enable and conserve', and provided themes for my later books in the 1980s and 1990s on *Future Work,*

12. All those aims will be supported by the money-system reforms proposed in the coming chapters. I believe that they will be more relevant to UK Prime Minister David Cameron's idea of the 'Big Society' than he himself yet recognises. 13. Bill Dyson, director of the Vanier Institute of the Family in Canada (1972-1983), who died in 1989, was a good friend who confirmed my understanding of pre-political action, and put us in touch with many other like-minded people in Canada. http://tinyurl.com/706d6h3.

Future Wealth, The New Economics of Sustainable Development and *Transforming Economic Life*.[14] Meanwhile, from 1975 to 2000 we were sending out a twice-yearly *Turning Point 2000* newsletter and organising regular *Turning Point 2000* events. These were not specifically about the future of money but often included items about it.[15]

By the mid-1980s, when Jonathon Porritt asked us to support him and Paul Ekins, Sara Parkin and their Green Party colleagues to set up The Other Economic Summit (TOES) in 1984, we were able to attract a good number of people to join us, and then to help to develop it into the New Economics Foundation (nef) in 1986.[16]

We have kept up a close connection with nef since then. Two papers I wrote for it in the 1990s were largely about money:

- a submission (1993) to the Independent International Commission On Global Governance, whose report was published in 1995 as *Our Global Neighbourhood*;
- and a paper on *Benefits and Taxes: A Radical Strategy* (1994).

My message in the Global Governance paper was that "as the world community begins to move – as it soon must – towards developing a global taxation system and a global monetary system, this will open up new possibilities for financing the activities of the UN". The 'Benefits and Taxes' paper explored a combination of key reforms in how governments raise public revenue and how they spend it – a shift to taxing land values and energy instead of taxing incomes, profits and value added, combined with the introduction of a Citizen's Income (basic income).[17]

Then in 2000, at an enthusiastic event at the National Portrait Gallery in London, nef's then director Ed Mayo[18] launched the publication of *Creating New Money: A Monetary Reform for the Information Age*[19] about how the money supply should be created and managed, written by Joseph Huber[20] and myself. At that event I gave nef's first 'Alternative Mansion House Speech'

---

14. See www.jamesrobertson.com/books.htm. 15. See www.jamesrobertson.com/turningpoint.htm. 16. For details see www.jamesrobertson.com/toes-nef.htm. 17. As previous reference. 18. Ed Mayo is now the Secretary General of Co-operatives UK, the membership network for co-operative businesses. 19. www.jamesrobertson.com/books.htm#creating.
20. www.soziologie.uni-halle.de/huber/index.en.html.

– on *Financial and Monetary Policies for an Enabling State.*[21]

So by 2000 the whole picture – national, local and international – was beginning to come into focus:

- how governments and government agencies carry out their three main money functions – providing the official money supply, raising public revenue, and spending it to meet public needs – heavily influence how the money system as a whole motivates people, businesses and countries to live our lives;
- how governments now carry out all three of those functions is badly out-of date; they motivate us to behave perversely, and need urgent reform;
- as a basis for their reform, we need to review what the purposes and principles of the money system should be as a whole, in order to meet the needs of human societies today; and
- its central purpose should be to motivate us and enable us to organise our personal and collective lives in ways that will lead, not to the self-destruction of our species, but to the survival and well-being of humankind and life on Earth.

Having explored that picture further in the past ten years or so has confirmed to me that few, if any, of the world's money professionals and policy-makers are interested in the purposes of how the whole money system works, or whether indeed it has any purposes. They do not seem to realise that how governments carry out their three main operational money functions is bound to motivate people to behave in some ways rather than others. They appear not to have the collective understanding or capacity to take forward an urgent, comprehensive programme of money-system reform.

They will have to be compelled to that by a growing force of informed public opinion and action. Protest will not be enough. Constructive leadership will be necessary too, focused on the practical measures needed to make the money system work better for the great majority of us than it works now. I hope this book will help to create a compelling force of that kind.

I have tried to avoid the financial jargon that obscures important simple facts. I have also tried to limit the use of statistics about how the money system works now. As the book will show, many of today's statistical series are based on today's money values, and those values are themselves based on

21. www.jamesrobertson.com/ne/alternativemansionhousespeech-2000.pdf.

questionable concepts that cloud our understanding of realities. So the book will mainly 'talk concepts rather than numbers'.[22] One aim of the book, apart from helping readers to see what needs to be done, is to help teachers preparing courses on the role of money in the new economy, by providing the range of information in Appendix 2 as well as in the main text of the book.

Finally, I have tried to keep the book short, concentrating on the core governmental functions dealing with money, which will determine whether or not the money system will meet its 21st-century purposes. Modernising those core functions will make it possible to reduce the present scale of corrective responses like public borrowing and complex financial regulation. For example, it will enable us to remove altogether from the national money system the malfunctioning extraneous growths like 'casino banking' that live off it today, and regulate them as we regulate the wide range of other forms of betting and gambling, including lotteries, and the results of horse-racing and other sporting activities.[23]

That, and other proposed structural changes, will accord with how the Copernican revolution eventually simplified our understanding of the relationship between our sun, ourselves and the other planets, and made it no longer necessary to compensate for its errors by a complex piling of epicycles on epicycles. But, as I said at the start of this Preface, the coming money-system revolution will not only be an *intellectual* one clarifying our understanding of how the money system works. If it is not already too late, it must also be a peaceful *practical* revolution modernising the money system to motivate us to act willingly in ways that will promote the survival and well-being of our species and life on Earth.

Comprehensive reform of the worldwide money system on those lines will be a necessary condition, if not by itself a sufficient one, for the survival of human society in its present form beyond the end of this century. Without it, we will continue to face the "world of mounting confusion and horror" that Ronald Higgins foresaw in 1978 in his brilliant book *The Seventh Enemy: The Human Factor in the Global Crisis*.[24] Whether or not we will be able to avoid that outcome of the human factor is now uncertain, but we have to try.

---

22. Stephen Zarlenga, director, American Monetary Institute, in recent personal correspondence. His book *The Lost Science of Money: The Mythology of Money – the Story of Power* is a masterwork. www.monetary.org. 23. See Chapter 3 for more on this point. 24. Ronald Higgins, *The Seventh Enemy: The Human Factor in the Global Crisis*, Hodder and Stoughton, 1978.

A summary of key points

1. Background

We may be destroying the ability of the Earth's resources to support our present way of life and even our survival as a species. Present recognition of that coincides with our having evolved a globalised money system that influences the way of life for almost everyone on Earth.

We need to understand that those two things are closely linked. How the money system works motivates us to live in some ways rather than others; how it now works motivates us to live in ways that not only treat most people unjustly but may also accelerate our suicide as a species; so we clearly need to decide what changes we must make in the ways the money system works.

In other words, we need a revolution of understanding *and* action:

(1) to achieve a less primitive level of *understanding* how the money system works, as the Copernican Revolution did for our understanding of the solar system; and then, on the basis of that new understanding,
(2) to identify and carry out *practical reforms* to change the way the money system works and bring money values more closely into line with human values and purposes in the 21st century.

2. Some lessons from the history of money (Chapter 1)

The unspoken purposes of the money system from its origins to the present time can be seen as being:

(1) to transfer wealth from poorer and weaker to richer and more powerful people and countries, and – as far as possible –
(2) to conceal this in mystery, myth and technical tricks of the trade.

In recent centuries two further purposes have evolved:

(3) to develop the technical, economic and military power of nations in competition with one another; and, in pursuing that aim
(4) to exploit the resources of the planet to the maximum extent.

3. The connection between money and ethics (Chapter 2)

The money system is a human invention. It reflects and embodies particular values and purposes. We must now decide how to change the way it works to embody new values and purposes that match our 21st-century needs.

Bringing it up to date will not only motivate us all to live differently. It will also enable us to use money values as a less misleading measure of achievement than 'economic growth' as we calculate it now.

4. The necessary reforms (Chapters 3-6)

Changing how the global money system works will involve reforming and developing how its national, international and local subsystems work. (We look at them in that order, because national money systems are now the most fully developed of the three, and because how they are reformed must give greater freedom to local communities to regenerate their local economies and money systems.)

5. Reform of national money systems (Chapters 3 and 4)

Governments are at the heart of the money system. By deciding

- how the national money supply is created,
- what is taxed and not taxed, and
- what public expenditure is spent on and not spent on,

governments largely determine where money goes as it flows through the economy, thereby influencing the impact of our activities on other people and the Earth's resources. The proposed reforms can be summarised as follows.

(1) Money supply (Chapter 3):

Transfer the function of creating the national money supply

(a) from commercial banks as a source of private profit to themselves,
(b) to a public agency – the central bank – as a source of debt-free public revenue to be spent into circulation by the government for public purposes.

(2) Taxation (Chapter 4):

(a) take taxes off incomes, profits, value added and other financial rewards for useful work and enterprise,
(b) put taxes on to value subtracted by people and organisations for private profit from common resources (such as land) and from the environment's capacity to absorb pollution and waste (such as carbon emissions); and
(c) reduce the present opportunities (through tax havens, etc) for rich people and businesses to avoid paying their dues to society.

(3) Public expenditure (Chapter 4)

(a) reduce public spending on perverse subsidies, and on some of the dependency-reinforcing services now provided directly by big government or by expensive contracts to big business and big finance, and
(b) transfer that money to the distribution of a Citizen's Income directly to all citizens, enabling them to decide how more of their rightful share in the value of common resources should be spent.

6. Development of the international money system (Chapter 5)

It should follow broadly the same lines as national money systems.

(1) Create a genuine international money supply, based on a new International Currency. It should replace the use of national superpower currencies for international trade and other international transactions, and operate in parallel with the continuing use of national currencies for transactions within their own boundaries.

(2) Develop arrangements for international revenue collection by taxing and charging:

(a) for the use of global commons, including ocean fishing, sea-bed mining, sea lanes, flight lanes, outer space and the electromagnetic spectrum, and
(b) for activities that pollute and damage the global environment, or cause hazards beyond national boundaries, such as emissions of CO_2 and CFCs, oil spills, and dumping wastes at sea.

(3) Rationalise and develop international public spending (from international revenue):

(a) to meet the costs of the expanding activities of the United Nations and its organisations, including international disaster relief and peacekeeping; and, if enough extra revenue is available,
(b) to distribute it on a per capita basis to every nation.

7. Local money systems (Chapter 6)

The regeneration of more self-reliant local economies will be essential to the human future in anything like its present form. Responding to local community needs, local governments will have an active part to play. But independent community currencies, local co-operatives, credit unions and development banks should be free to participate actively.

8. Are these reforms achievable? (Conclusion)

They could be achieved. But whether they are will depend on us.

Note: Readers will find that many of these key points are repeated in various parts of the book. This recognises that I see the different reform proposals in relation to one another, as integrated parts of a reformed money system.

PART ONE

Understanding the money system

Summary

Part One consists of:

The *Introduction* – to the system of money that has now developed worldwide to motivate everyone to live their lives in some ways rather than others; that is now motivating all of us – rich and poor alike – to live in ways that threaten the future of our civilisation; and that now calls urgently for reform;

Chapter 1 – on lessons from the history of money, illustrating how piecemeal changes over the centuries have left us with a muddled money system today, with purposes that directly conflict with 21st-century needs; and

Chapter 2 – on ethics, money values and real-life values, and the new purposes needed for the money system.

These prepare the way for the practical proposals in Part Two for the comprehensive reform now needed for our worldwide money system as it works today.

PART ONE

Introduction: the evolving money system

Understanding money as an evolving system[1]

Over the centuries the world's money systems have been evolving into a single worldwide system.

Flows of money now connect comparatively well developed *national money systems* based on their own currencies (or a currency like the euro that serves a group of nations) with

- externally, a less fully developed *international money system*, still based on no genuine currency of its own, and
- internally, varying numbers of relatively small, less fully developed *local money systems*, in some cases using a 'complementary' local currency like Totnes Pounds or Ithaca Hours for exchanging limited ranges of local goods and services, not nearly as closely connected with one another as national money systems now are.

The message of this book is that, assuming it is not already too late, further evolution of the whole worldwide money system is urgently needed, involving:

- a restructuring of national money systems, and a reduction of their present centralising power;
- further development of the international money system and local money systems; and

1. Roy Madron and John Jopling take an interestingly different 'systems approach' in *Gaian Democracies: Redefining Globalisation & People-Power*, Schumacher Briefing No 9, Green Books, 2003. Readers may like to compare their approach with mine.

- the purposeful evolution of them all into a global system that serves the various common interests of all the world's people more effectively, democratically and ecologically than the global system serves us today.

The behaviour of almost everyone on Earth, with its effects on the lives of other people and the natural world, is now motivated to a great extent by how the money system works. We need to understand:

- how that process of motivation happens;
- how it is now motivating us to behave in ways that threaten our future;
- how to change the way it works; and
- what we can do to make sure it is changed that way.

Many otherwise intelligent people think that how the money system works is too difficult for them to understand. One of the lessons of its history (Chapter 1) is that the people responsible for developing and managing the money system since its origins up to the present day have encouraged that sense of mystery. When we are convinced that the way the system now works must be changed, it becomes easier to understand why it now works so badly and therefore how it needs to be changed. As the German philosopher Johann Gottlieb Fichte (1762-1814) put it, "We do not act because we know. We know because we are called upon to act."[2]

Like every system, the money system is composed of elements of various kinds which work together. We don't have to understand in great detail how all the elements work, just that they combine to make the system work the way it does. The elements include:

- ***different kinds of participant***, including
  (a) people and households,
  (b) localities and local governmental agencies,
  (c) countries and national governments and their agencies,
  (d) international governmental agencies,
  (e) multinational business and finance corporations,
  (f) small companies, and
  (g) other non-governmental organisations, including co-operatives, community enterprises and charities operating locally, nationally and internationally;

2. See http://brooklynrail.org/notefrompub and other internet references to Fichte.

- ***different functions***, like creating and managing the supply of money, and taxing, earning, spending, lending, borrowing, investing and giving money;
- ***different currencies***: national currencies like the dollar, the euro, the pound, the yen or the renminbi/yuan;[3] and local, alternative, complementary or community currencies, used in parallel with the national currencies of the countries in which they exist; and
- ***different technologies***, such as gold or silver or other metal coins, or paper notes, or electronic data held in computers and transmitted between them.

Elements of the money system			
Participants	**Functions**	**Currencies**	**Technologies**
People/ households Local govts National govts International govt agencies Multinational corporations National businesses Small companies NGOs, charities etc	Creating & managing money supplies Taxing Earning Spending Lending Borrowing Investing Giving	Multinational National Local	Metal coins Paper notes Electronic data

Those different participants, functions, currencies and technologies combine to make the money system work:

- as a worldwide system distributing flows of money to different people and organisations in different nations, and through them to other people and organisations and nations;
- as a calculus with which we compare the money values of different things and different activities with one another;
- as a scoring system that decides the value of the claims that people and organisations and countries are entitled to make on others in exchange for goods and services; and
- therefore as a system that rewards some activities and penalises others, motivating people and organisations and countries everywhere to behave in some ways rather than others – depending on how we make the money system work.

---

3. In the present absence of a genuine international currency, some of these are now also used for international transactions.

How money operates as a motivating system	
SYSTEM FOR DISTRIBUTING MONEY FLOWS	Distribution of flows of money to different people and organisations in different nations, and through them to other people and organisations and nations
CALCULUS SYSTEM	Means of comparing the money values of different things and different activities with one another
SCORING SYSTEM	Means of deciding the value of the claims that people and organisations and countries are entitled to make on others in exchange for goods and services
REWARD AND MOTIVATION SYSTEM	A system for rewarding some activities and penalising others, thereby motivating people, organisations and countries everywhere to behave in some ways rather than others

Money is a human invention

That the money system is a human invention is obvious, but it must be kept in mind. We must not allow ourselves to be persuaded that "there is no alternative" (TINA)[4] to how it works at present.

Up to a point we can compare the money system with other manmade systems that govern flows of natural resources like water and energy. Water, for example, is captured from a source, say a river or a reservoir, and distributed to intermediate centres which control its distribution to subsidiary centres and so on until the water reaches its final users. If we find, after installing irrigation systems or other water systems, that the flows of water through them could be changed for the better, nobody would claim that in principle there is no alternative to the present pattern of flows we have installed – although there may be practical difficulties on the ground.

However, money is not even a natural resource like water. We don't find money in Nature. The behaviour of animals, birds, fishes, insects, plants, trees and rocks does not involve exchanges of money of any kind. Their behaviour is not affected by money – except by how humans are motivated by money.

4. Mrs Thatcher's belief as British Prime Minister in the 1980s.

So no law of nature explains or dictates how the money system works. The worldwide loss of trillions of dollars in the financial crisis of the past few years, which still continues to become more and more threatening, can't be blamed on a tsunami or an earthquake. It may be true that nobody responsible for managing the money system seems to know how much was lost, or where it went to, or where it originally came from, or indeed what to do about it. But everyone knows that the crash and its aftermath have not been due to uncontrollable natural causes, but to a human design and management failure of monumental proportions. The fact that we have so far been unable to pin responsibility for it on anyone in particular is simply a measure of the incompetence and irresponsibility, primarily of our leaders but therefore also of ourselves. We are a supposedly intelligent species, but cannot control the outcomes of the clever systems we invent.[5]

Money is, in fact, an immaterial manmade resource.[6] Flows of money carry claims to numerical money values exchangeable for other things. The bigger the value of the flows of money we receive as people and organisations and countries, the more freedom it will give us to use other resources. The smaller the value of the money flows we receive, the more limited will be our ability to use other resources. Flows of money to us bring economic power and freedom; lack of money flowing to us brings economic poverty.

How the money system works to determine the patterns of money flowing through society depends on how we make it work. How it works is what now needs to be changed. In principle we can perfectly well change it, as our predecessors have continually done in the past, to meet the changing needs and purposes of their times according to their own interests.[7]

Unfortunately, the managers of the money system up to the present time have been so committed to make it work in their own interests and have made so many piecemeal changes in it to that end, that the whole picture is now one of total confusion. Nobody seems to think about how the whole system works, what its purposes are, what its purposes should be, and how it should be designed and managed to achieve them.

That is why our present primitive understanding of the money system is like the pre-Copernican understanding of the solar system. We need a new understanding of how the money system works, like the new Copernican

5. Some people will see deep-sea oil drilling and nuclear power as two other examples. 6. See Chapter 7 for the role of gold and other commodities in the money system. 7. For the past, see Chapter 1; for changes now proposed, see Chapters 3 to 6.

understanding of the solar system. And then we face a challenge that Copernicus and his followers like Kepler did not have to face. We have to decide what new purposes the money system *should have*, and how *we should change* its present ways of working to adapt it to those new purposes.

In other words, this 'new Copernican revolution' will involve an *intellectual* breakthrough on which a *practical* modernisation programme can be based:[8]

- the *intellectual* breakthrough will be as simple as understanding that the Earth goes round the sun, not vice versa; it will be to understand that we humans have developed the money system as an instrument for achieving human purposes;
- the practical modernisation programme can then be based on our answers to the following questions:

(1) what should the 21st-century purposes of the money system be? and
(2) what changes should we make in the way it now works, to match it to those purposes?

Why comparing money values motivates our behaviour

We use the term 'money values' here in a concrete sense, because it refers to the actual numbers of units of particular currencies that indicate the price or cost of particular activities and things at particular places at particular times. How our governments make the money system work in that respect combines with other things – like prevailing conditions of demand and supply – to put different values on different activities and things compared with others. That way it provides a scoring system for human activities and our economic products and exchanges.

How that scoring system motivates us to behave in some ways rather than others can be understood in a simple way by seeing how changing the scoring

---

8. Some implications of this are discussed in Chapters 2 and 4. I have already mentioned in the Preface the interesting parallel between our understanding of the money system and our understanding of the solar system. Complicated and costly corrections have had to be introduced to compensate for failings in our unreformed mainstream money system, which correspond to the complications of 'epicycles piled on epicycles' that had to be introduced into late Ptolemaic astronomy to explain why the paths of the planets supposedly circling the Earth – and subsequently the sun – did not move in simple circles. See Sir James Jeans, *Physics and Philosophy*, Cambridge University Press, 1942, pages 184-5.

system affects less important and less complicated games. The players are motivated to play the game differently when changes in the scoring system change the rewards and penalties attaching to the outcomes of the game's various activities. For example, in football giving three points (instead of two points) for a win and one point for a draw in tables of results can motivate players to play for a win; and in rugby football raising the value of a try to five points plus a score of two points for a successful 'conversion' kick at goal can motivate players to score tries instead of kicking either penalty goals or drop goals for three points.

By determining prices, money provides a scoring system that motivates us as strongly as almost any other. It doesn't just record what has happened; in continuing to play the game and live our lives, we have to depend on spending the scores we have previously got. So, in order to motivate us collectively to change how we now treat our fellow humans and other species and the natural resources on which we depend, we must change the ways the money system now results in comparative money values that encourage us to behave in ways that threaten our survival.

Changing the ways governments handle their own flows of money inevitably plays the central part. The reform proposals in Chapters 3 to 6 deal with that in more detail. The background is as follows.

Governments can't avoid deciding how money works

One way or another, consciously or not, governments can't help deciding how the money system works.

They and their agencies have three primary responsibilities for dealing with money:

- deciding who should create and manage the national *money supply*, and in what form – for example public agencies creating it debt-free in the public interest, or commercial banks creating it as interest-bearing debt profitable to themselves (Chapter 3);
- raising national *public revenue* – and deciding, for example, what is to be taxed and what is not to be taxed (Chapter 4); and
- managing national *public spending* – and deciding what the public revenue should be spent on and what it should not be spent on (also Chapter 4).

How those three functions are carried out has a dominating effect on the flows of money through the economy as a whole, and on the relative money values of almost all our activities and everything we buy and sell:

(a) Whoever creates the money supply and puts it into circulation in what form – whether as interest-paying debt or free of debt – will direct the initial flows of money in favour of some recipients and activities rather than others, and that will have after-effects that influence money values as the money continues to circulate through the economy.
(b) *Taxes* now take at least a third of the money value of total economic activity from some activities, and *public spending* then puts it back into others. Taxes add to the costs of what they tax, while public spending reduces the costs of what it supports. What is taxed and what is not taxed, together with what public money is spent on and what it is not spent on, cannot avoid resulting in money values that strongly favour some people and some activities at the expense of others in every part of the economy.
(c) The combined outcomes of those three functions affect the prices of everything in the economy – even things that, although not themselves taxed or subsidised, benefit or suffer in comparison with those that are.

That set of fairly simple facts leads us to the following conclusions.

First, it means that any idea of the money system providing 'objective values' or 'a level playing field' is sheer fantasy. And that means that democratic governments and a democratic world society should deliberately organise and manage their overall flows of money to motivate how citizens and businesses and nations deal with *their* money. Common sense suggests that we should all be motivated to deal with it in ways that, while serving our own interests, will automatically serve the interests of others too – instead of damaging them. Being so simple, that key point about how the 21st-century money system could and should work has so far escaped expert understanding!

Second, if those three primary money functions of governments:

- *providing the national money supply,*
- *raising the public revenue* and
- *spending on public purposes*

were designed and managed efficiently as a self-balancing whole, they would minimise the need for governments' two corrective money functions:

- *borrowing money for public purposes* and
- *regulating the activities of private sector financial enterprises* like banks.

As things are, however, those fourth and fifth money functions of governments – borrowing money for public purposes and regulating private-sector financial activities – continue to grow more complex and costly year by year.

Primary and corrective money functions of governments
PRIMARY MONEY FUNCTIONS
Providing the national money supply
Raising the public revenue
Spending on public purposes
CORRECTIVE MONEY FUNCTIONS
Borrowing money for public purposes
Regulating the activities of private sector financial enterprises

Third, as the problems of government, banking and general indebtedness continue to develop further in the eurozone and the wider world, and as understanding grows that the present level of indebtedness will never be paid back as long as the money needed to pay it back continues to be created as debt for private-sector profit, we should replace that way of creating it with another.

Through the centuries, many attempts have been made in various parts of world to shake off the burdens of debt, as under Solon's leadership in 6th-century-BC Athens (see Chapter 1). But what success they may have had has been only temporary. The wealth gap – which is now at a dangerous level in modern societies – between those who suffer from debt and those who profit from it has always grown again. The obvious long-term solution to the problem will be to deprive commercial banks of the privilege of providing the money supply as profit-making debt and transfer to a public agency the function of creating it debt-free on the lines proposed in Chapter 3; and to combine that with the proposed shifts in taxation and public spending in Chapter 4.

Fourth, a spiralling burden of unproductive governmental and financial administrative superstructures, feeding off one another and the rest of society, may have played a key part in the collapse of past civilisations. For example, Joseph Tainter cites "investment in complexity" as a cause of the collapse of the late Roman Empire.[9] Could the growing economic, social and ecological burdens of debt and administrative costs of financial services and their regulation contribute to the collapse of our world society today?

That brings us to the future prospects for the well-being and survival of our civilisation, and perhaps even of our species.

The prospects for our civilisation

Distinguished scientists already believe that the present century may well be "our final century",[10] that "homo sapiens will become extinct, perhaps within 100 years",[11] and that the "face of Gaia" is already vanishing.[12] One of many well-informed recent appraisals is the 2008 paper by the International Environment Forum on 'Preventing Overshoot and Collapse: Managing the Earth's Resources'.[13] Another is the 2011 assessment from the Future Planet Research Centre following Japan's "triple major disaster of the monster earthquake, tsunami, and nuclear meltdown".[14] But nobody can yet forecast accurately when the collapse of our civilisation may become irreversible.

It is not one of the aims of this book to assess the chances of our civilisation collapsing by the end of this century. But, if we cannot rule out the possibility of this happening during the lifetime of toddlers alive today, and we realise that how our money system now works in ways that will help to make it happen – we will be very short-sighted if we fail to give top priority to reforming the way the money system now works.

---

9. *The Collapse of Complex Societies*, Cambridge University Press, 1988, pp. 148-152. 10. Professor Martin Rees, *Our Final Century: Will the Human Race Survive the Twenty-First Century?* Heinemann 2003. The Astronomer Royal believes we have only a 50/50 chance of surviving into the next century. 11. Professor Frank Fenner, emeritus professor of microbiology at the Australian National University, believes "it's an irreversible situation. I think it's too late." See http://tinyurl.com/7fo2kqe. 12. James Lovelock, *The Vanishing Face of Gaia*, Allen Lane, 2009. 13. http://iefworld.org/ddahlo8d.htm. 14. http://tinyurl.com/7mpmabb.

Only connect[15]

As will be clear from Chapter 1, the history of the money system from its origins to the present day shows that the people in charge of it over the centuries have been guided by two main tacit purposes that are badly out of date:

- to transfer money, wealth, power and well-being from poor people and countries to rich ones; and, since the industrial revolution,
- to encourage maximum extraction and exploitation of natural resources.

Hitherto those two main purposes have implicitly guided the piecemeal changes that our rulers and their financial associates have made in the money system over the centuries in response to problems and opportunities as they arose. It is now becoming clear, not only that the way the money system now works is out of keeping with our more democratic age, but that it is motivating us all to conduct our lives in ways that could lead to the extinction of our species. Nonetheless, the piecemeal approach continues to dominate its development and to ignore the need to consider how the way it works as a whole should be transformed to meet the needs and purposes of today.

An outcome of this is clearly seen at the global level by the recent series of UN conferences in Copenhagen, Cancun and Durban on what to do about the crisis of the world's changing climate, and the separate series of G20 (Group of 20) conferences on what to do about the crisis of the world's financial system. The politicians, officials and experts involved in each of those series of conferences appear to have come from largely unconnected universes of thought and action, and to have been largely unaware of the relevance to one another of what each may eventually decide.

That is linked to the fact that we have organisations meant to deal with international money questions – the International Monetary Fund (IMF), World Bank, and Bank for International Settlements (BIS) – that have operated quite separately from the United Nations (UN) agencies that deal with almost everything else. An unintended result of that is that one outstanding ecological issue – how the international community should develop ways of using money to cope with global climate change – is now being dealt with under the UN quite separately from an equally vital connected issue – how the international financial community should reform the way that the inter-

15. I agree with Helen Clarkson of Forum for the Future, www.forumforthefuture.org/blog/only-connect, that E.M. Forster's advice "Only connect" in *Howard's End* (1910) "is possibly one of the best explanations of sustainability I know. Sustainability is not just, after all, about environment, economics, and society, but about the linkages between those fields and how they affect one another."

national money system works, which has led us into the still continuing global financial crisis of the past few years.

Those organisational disconnections reflect and strengthen a contradiction we are now trying live with: on the one hand we need to adapt the money system to a new purpose of securing the survival and well-being of our species and life on Earth in a more democratic world society; on the other hand our established leaders are aiming to restore the money system to its old purpose of promoting conventionally measured, money-maximising economic growth led by rich people and countries in their own interest. This 'cognitive dissonance' will only be resolved by a clearer view of what the money system should be for, as a basis for its practical development to serve its new purposes.

However, before pursuing that further we should recognise the overriding need to simplify how the system works. It will not be enough just to avoid making its workings more complicated than they are now. We need to make them drastically simpler and easier for those who manage them to manage them efficiently, and for everyone else to see how well or badly they are doing it.

Money must be made to work more simply and clearly

Various reasons for the present widespread ignorance about how the money system works and how it could be changed for the better will become clear from future chapters.

One is simply that over the centuries the people in charge of it have responded to different problems and opportunities with piecemeal changes off-the-cuff, rather than with planned modifications to any existing overall plan or design. This has led to a money system in a continually expanding state of muddle. Just as Sir Robert Morant, a notable administrator in the early 20th century, described the obsolete structures of British government then, the money system now is like the result of someone "seeking to build a substantial house by working spasmodically on odd portions of the structure on quite isolated plans, fashioning minute details of some upper parts, when he has not set up, nor indeed even planned out, the substructure which is their sole foundation and stay: his very best efforts being rendered abortive by the fact that, while he is hammering at this portion of it or that, he possesses no clearly thought-out plan of the structure as a whole."[16]

It is hard to deny that the money system has been allowed to grow into a more or less unmanageable mess. One of many typical everyday illustrations was the recent discovery by the UK Coalition Government that both the system of personal taxes (that transfer money from citizens to the state) and the system of personal benefits and tax credits (that transfer money from the state to citizens) had grown up little by little over the years separately from one another, and that merging them now into a purposefully integrated and easily understandable system has become almost impossible.[17]

Another reason why it is difficult to understand how the money system works and how it needs to be changed is that almost all the policymakers in government and public finance have been conditioned to accept that it is preferable for the public not to understand it. That is partly a simple throwback to the time when the money system was managed by monarchs (and their associates) for their own purposes. But there has also been anxiety that, in a parliamentary democracy, widespread understanding of how the money system works might create irresistible public pressure on elected Members of Parliament to vote in the short-term financial interests of their own constituencies rather than in the longer-term interests of the electorate at large. For example, Lord Turner, who has more recently been seen as a progressive chairman of the UK Financial Services Authority, insisted – before the present continuing crisis broke in 2007-08 – that "non-transparent money creation" is "based on well founded fears that governments will abuse direct control of money printing presses".[18] Safeguards against this possibility are proposed in Chapter 3. But there are other reasons for this reticence too.

One has been to avoid revealing that, as will be clear from the following chapters, the overall effect of how the money system works still benefits the rich at the expense of the poor, as in pre-democratic times. Another is that having a money system that is difficult to understand is profitable for the professionals – including the officials, bankers, accountants and lawyers, who make their living from managing it, providing its services, and

---

16. James Robertson, *Reform of British Central Government*, Chatto & Windus and Charles Knight, 1971, p 5. 17. To follow this up in detail, see Chapter 5 of the 2010 Mirrlees Review at http://tinyurl.com/84tuy9r. For critical comment, see Richard Murphy's http://tinyurl.com/7jzmj4j. 18. Adair Turner, 'Europe's Best Defence Against Deflation', *Financial Times*, 4 November 2002.

advising people and businesses and governments how to use it in their own interests.[19]

As I have mentioned, the last two of governments' five main money functions – borrowing and regulation – can be seen to have developed as corrective responses to failures in the other three. As the history of money shows,[20] the first three (providing the money supply, raising the public revenue, and spending it on public purposes) have often proved unable to meet the needs of governments as they have arisen. Borrowing and regulating have then been used as correctives to fill those gaps.

There are clear signs now that failure to define 21st-century purposes for the money system as a whole could lead to a whole new range of complication and confusion. It arises from the assumption that a new area of financial activity operating outside governments' three mainstream money functions (money supply, taxes and public spending) is needed to deal with climate change – and presumably in future many other new environmental challenges too. It consists of a new range of profit-based rationing and trading schemes,[21] for example for carbon emissions under the Kyoto Protocol. None of these so far appears to have achieved the aim of reducing carbon emissions. At least some, like the EU Carbon Emissions Trading Scheme, have given sizeable windfall profits to heavily polluting companies.[22] Others are no more than scams.[23]

In bringing the money system up to date to encourage ecologically, socially and economically desirable behaviour, we should be very careful not to complicate it unnecessarily with a jungle of special schemes that make it more difficult for all concerned to understand how the system should work as a whole, and easier for the financial professionals to cheat everyone.

As far as we possibly can, we should achieve the changes we need to make for those and other new purposes by bringing up to date the operations of the mainstream financial functions of national and international governments and government agencies – to provide the money supply, collect the public revenue, and spend it on public purposes. Otherwise, we will simply enlarge the opportunities for unprincipled financial practitioners to rip us off.[24]

---

19. See, for example, this *Telegraph* article about the "bonanza for city lawyers, advisers and accountants": http://tinyurl.com/yegymzq. 20. See Chapter 1. For example, the Bank of England owes its origin in 1694 to the inability of King William III to raise money by taxation for his wars with France. 21. Known as 'cap and trade', 'cap and share', 'quota trading', etc. 22. See the *Telegraph* article on the windfalls from EU carbon trading: http://tinyurl.com/yjhw8mw.
23. http://tinyurl.com/30gh6xj. 24. See Chapter 7 for more on this.

Purposes for the money system in the 21st century

The aspirations of people all over the world for greater political and economic democracy, freedom and justice are growing. We are also becoming rapidly more aware of the need to shift to ecologically conserving ways of life that will enable our own species and others to survive in decent conditions. So it makes sense to explore the possibility that the right purposes for a reformed money system will be on the following lines:

- to enable everyone to benefit from organising the production and exchange of goods and services as fairly and freely and efficiently as possible, and
- to motivate us all to live and organise our lives in ways that maintain the planet's resources in conditions supportive to the survival and well-being of our species and life on Earth.

It also makes sense to explore whether the following arrangements might best meet those purposes:

- the public money supply should be created and put into circulation by public agencies serving the common interest;
- people and businesses should be rewarded untaxed for the value of what we contribute by our efforts and skills to the value of common resources, the common wealth and the common well-being;
- people and businesses should pay taxes (or charges) on the value of what we take from those common resources and the common wealth for our own benefit, and
- we should all have a share of the resulting revenue, in the form of a citizen's income;
- those arrangements should motivate us to meet our own needs in ways that help others to meet theirs, and to conserve our common inheritance of the world's resources;
- they should not restrict our freedoms unnecessarily;
- in fact they should positively encourage groups of people or companies to participate in local complementary currencies and co-operatively managed enterprises, provided that those don't cause injustice to others; and finally

- governments should change the way the money system works to make it easier for people to 'downsize' their use of money, to enable us to provide goods and services for ourselves and our families by our own work – in contrast to the way it now works to make us increasingly dependent on getting money to meet our needs.[25]

25. The introduction of a universal Citizen's Income will play a particular part in this. A more general point to note is that these new freedoms from the centralising effects of Big Money, as from those of Big Government and Big Business, will be crucial to the 'Big Society' idea of UK Prime Minister David Cameron. See www.communities.gov.uk/communities/bigsociety. For a 25-year-old view on what is now being called the 'Big Society', see *Future Work* at www.jamesrobertson.com/books.htm#futurework.

CHAPTER 1

Some lessons from the history of money[1]

This chapter summarises in broad chronological order the evolving historical background to the proposals in Chapters 3-6 for changing how the money system now works.

It shows that, from the origin of the money system until now, two of its main purposes have been: to transfer wealth and well-being to powerful and rich people and countries, from weaker and poorer ones; and to veil – in mystery, deceit and cheating – how that is done.

In recent centuries in Europe and subsequently worldwide, those two purposes of the money system have combined to develop new capabilities for a third and fourth: to exploit the resources of the planet; and to develop the technical, economic and military power of competing nations.

We have now reached a tipping point. We can see that by our exploitation of the planet's resources, by our unjust competition between people and between nations, and by our relentless development of ever more lethal technologies, we are likely to destroy our civilisation in the foreseeable future. At the same time, we are beginning to see that the way the money system now works drives us to continue on that course.

The origins of money

Archaeologists may have found older traces of coins in China and elsewhere, but the lessons we can draw from the history of money start with the early

---

1. This chapter is largely based on material prepared for *Une Histoire de l'Argent: des origines à nos jours*, published by Autrement, Paris, November 2007. See http://tinyurl.com/7q8fmo6. I am very grateful to Philippe Godard for his editorial support on that short book, and to Autrement for their permission to use the material here.

'bank accounts' for grain and other commodities given as tribute to ancient temples and palaces in Babylon and Egypt, followed by the gold and silver coins minted by rulers in Ionian Greece in the 8th to 6th centuries BC.

The myth of the god Bacchus giving King Midas the gift of turning everything he touched into gold; the Delphic oracle's equally disastrous advice that misled King Croesus, the richest man in the world, into losing his empire and fortune; and the priestly warning 'Outsiders, keep out'[2] – all these have helped to set the pattern that we have today for how the money system works. Unless we urgently change how it works as Euro-American world supremacy continues to decline, our legacy to humanity will include an unsustainable money system veiled in modern mystery and myth that leads us all towards the decline of our civilisation.

In the 18th century, as the industrial revolution took off, the Scottish Enlightenment philosopher Adam Smith[3] suggested that money owed its origins to merchants and bankers, rather than to rulers and priests. He noted that human nature has "a propensity to truck, barter and exchange" which is "to be found in no other race of animals". The growth of trade and the 'division of labour' between specialists in different skills, jobs and careers, gave profitable opportunities to merchants and bankers to develop money as a means of exchange more efficient and convenient than barter.

Today the money system works as a collaboration between rulers and commercial profit-making businesses. In our supposedly democratic societies, big governments and powerful financial and business corporations collaborate to shield money's workings from the understanding of citizens. With modern myths and magic about the need for never-ending money-measured 'economic growth', the way they manage the world's money makes us all increasingly dependent on the money they create and control.

The legacy of ancient Greece and Rome

As gold and silver coins spread through the city states of Greece, stamped with the emblems of their cities, Athens grew in power and wealth. Its famous 'owl of Minerva' coins were minted of silver, dug by thousands of short-lived slaves in the mines of Laurion. As Xenophon said, "The Divine Bounty has bestowed upon us inexhaustible mines of silver, and advantages which we

---

2. "Procul, O procul este, profani." Virgil, *Aeneid* vi, 256. 3. In *The Wealth of Nations*, 1776.

"ALL I HAVE LEARNED,
I LEARNED FROM BOOKS."

ABRAHAM LINCOLN

enjoy above all our neighbouring cities." Precious metals (gold and silver) were already playing their central part in the history of money, based on the assumption that 'real money' consisted of them or of the ability to exchange it for them. Since then, human lives have been sacrificed to gold and silver mining in almost every part of the world.

At the height of her empire in the 5th century BC, Athens compelled her allies to use her 'owl of Minerva' coins, and Athenian citizens had to hand over foreign coins to be recycled as 'owls'. This was profitable for Athens, and the money system continues to operate that way today. Unless they give it away, anyone who creates new money will profit from the difference between its value and the cost of producing it. Other people can only get it in exchange for providing goods and services such as work or by paying interest for borrowing it. Those who mainly profit are the rulers and commercial bankers who create the money in general use. Those from a country whose money is used in international as well as domestic exchanges of goods and services profit additionally from its use by people from other countries. Britain and then the US have occupied that dominating position in the past two centuries, as the pound and then the dollar have been used as the main international currency.

Throughout money's history the links between money and land and debt have been centrally important. More and more peasant farmers in Athens around 600 BC went more and more deeply into debt. Unable to meet their debts after bad harvests, they had to hand over their land to rich landowners and sometimes even to hand themselves over as slaves. The wise lawgiver, Solon, who had advised Croesus to call no man happy until he is dead, introduced reforms known as *Seisactheia*, the Greek word for 'shaking off the burdens'. This was an example of 'jubilee', reflecting the instruction said to have been given to Moses by God that, when the people of Israel had settled in their promised land, they should proclaim a jubilee every fifty years – a year to be joyful. Debts should be forgiven, every family who had lost their land should have it back, and every citizen who had become a slave should be freed. Similar 'Clean Slate' proclamations are said to have been made from time to time in Babylon and other ancient societies too.

The Jubilee idea became alive again much more recently. Jubilee 2000 was a worldwide campaign of over 20 million people that urged world leaders to celebrate the year 2000 by cancelling $100 billion of debts owed by poor countries to rich ones. The campaign received wide publicity and support, and as a result some debts of the poorest countries were cancelled.

But cancelling some existing debts, whether those of poor people or poor countries, can only be a palliative of temporary value if the money system continues to operate in ways that automatically transfer money from poor to rich; and so it has proved. Looking forward now from 2012, a comprehensive worldwide shaking-off of the existing worldwide burden of debt appears to be growing more necessary and possible. It is an open question whether a total collapse in the world's present money system – dwarfing the great crash of 1929 and the Great Depression of the 1930s – will be an eventual consequence of the continuing financial crisis triggered by irresponsible banking in 2007-8, or whether a planned 'decolonisation' of debt can be achieved.

As Rome expanded its rule over the whole of Italy and Greece and most of the then known world, it became much richer than Greece had been. The Roman Empire developed a sophisticated money-changing and banking system, linked to a network of tax collectors like St Matthew. The gap between rich and poor grew wider. Some Romans like Crassus, an older contemporary of Julius Caesar and Pompey, became as rich as today's multi-billionaires.

Ancient Greece and ancient Rome both showed a tendency over the years for a powerful minority to own most of the money and land. The Roman Empire in particular showed that a growing gap between a rich land-owning minority and a poor landless urban majority may ultimately help to bring about a society's collapse. As the city of Rome became crowded with thousands of landless people who could not earn their livelihoods, writers of the time – like Pliny (23-79 AD) and Juvenal (60-130 AD) – observed that the great landed estates were destroying the country. All that many Roman citizens spent their time on was free 'bread and circuses'. At the same time, the complexities of bureaucratic administration, tax gathering, debt and money-lending imposed increasingly heavy burdens on productive enterprise. Today, researchers into the collapse of past civilisations include those complexities as part of the cause of the late Roman Empire's failure to resist the waves of Franks, Vandals, Huns, Goths and other tribes from Northern Europe and Asia that overran its boundaries, leading to its break-up and the Dark Ages that followed.[4] Could world society today be on a similar path to an even more final disaster?

---

4. e.g. Joseph Tainter – see Introduction, footnote 9.

From feudalism to the revival of money

The Emperor Charlemagne (742-814) minted coins of silver dug from mines in Germany by slaves. These coins were modelled on the old Roman denarius. In France, 'denier' coins were used until the French Revolution. Pounds, shillings and pence were used in Britain until the 1970s; the shorthand for them was £sd; and the 'd' still stood for denarius.

In spite of this link with the Roman past, the feudal societies that emerged from the Dark Ages were organised around land in a network of reciprocal responsibilities, rather than around money. Dukes, barons and other nobles owed services to their king in exchange for their lands. Lower landowners owed services to those above them. At the bottom of the ladder, farmers and villagers and serfs owed services to their local landlords. An important service to the king was to provide men for his armies. Other farmers, villagers and serfs had to give their landlords a share of the produce from their land – meat, cloth, wheat, fruit, and so on – and work on their estates, building roads, cutting trees and harvesting and transporting crops.

Over the following centuries, payment of money steadily replaced the obligation to provide goods and services. It became the common understanding that subjects should pay taxes to kings and rulers, and people should pay rents to their landlords and earn wages for working. In general, the importance of money in almost all aspects of life has continued to grow right up to the present time. It has brought freedom and well-being for many people but has damaged and destroyed the lives of many others. More and more of us in more and more countries have become dependent on big employers to organise our work and provide our incomes, on big corporations to provide us with the necessities of life in exchange for our money, on big government to provide us with more and more services in exchange for more and more taxes, and on big banks to provide us with our societies' money supplies.

From about 1000 AD, countries like England, France and Spain began to be consolidated into nations, under rulers who strengthened their rule through their control of money. Important money functions for governments today have grown out of that, including: the creation and issue of money; the collection of tax money by rulers to spend on their needs and activities, especially wars; and, in the past few centuries, government spending on public needs. In the past thousand years those functions have developed piecemeal over time, in response to changing pressures on rulers and new opportunities for financial business.

Providing society with money

Money has been created in various ways. Rulers have minted it as coins which they have spent into circulation. Bankers have created it to lend to their customers, either as banknotes or simply by writing it into their customers' accounts as 'credit'; and members of local groups have themselves created money in 'complementary currencies' in exchange for goods and services provided by other members of the group. In every case, whoever creates new money gets a profit or a benefit from it. In today's democracies, the questions include: who profits, and who should profit, from creating official-currency money like the dollar, the euro and the pound?

In medieval times, providing the money supply meant minting coins and putting them into circulation by spending them. The power and wealth of rulers depended partly on whether their money was widely used by people in their own and other countries. For example, in the 13th century, King Louis IX of France (St Louis) ordered his subjects to use his coins for making payments throughout his kingdom – as the 5th-century-BC Athenian government had done.

Rulers profited from producing coins of greater value than the cost of minting them. Such profit is called seignorage, and it still applies today to the small part of the money supply that consists of coins and banknotes. In Britain that is now only about 3%, because our government allows the commercial banks to create the other 97% out of thin air in the form of profit-making loans which they write into their customers' bank accounts as 'credit'.

History is full of ways by which rich and powerful people have tricked money out of people. In the past, rulers could increase their seignorage profits by surreptitiously reducing the value of the gold or silver contained in the coins they minted. This was known as debasing the coinage. Henry VIII of England (1509-1547) is one of many rulers who did it. He is best remembered for having had six wives, having replaced the Pope as head of the Church of England, and having 'dissolved' the monasteries. But he also made everyone give him back their silver coins for new copper coins, covered with a thin surface of silver to make them look genuine. Unfortunately, when the silver coating wore off the King's nose on the coins, people could see that he was cheating them, and they nicknamed him 'Old Copper Nose'.

In those distant days when coins of gold and silver were the main vehicles for money, debasing them and clipping bits off them were among the main ways of deceiving and cheating people over money. Later, as paper money became more important than coins, and then electronic money became more important than banknotes, other tricks became more important.

Transforming taxes into acceptable charges

Taxes originated as tribute to rulers and priests in prehistoric societies. They are as old as money itself. After the Dark Ages and the feudal period, rulers revived taxes to provide them with money to spend on wars, road-building and other purposes – including spending on their palaces, servants, entertainments and other personal expenses. Only much later when more democratic societies began to emerge did people start thinking that public spending to meet the needs of society should be distinct from private spending on the personal needs of rulers.

Taxes have always been unpopular, which is why rulers have looked for other ways of raising money, like debasing the currency, seizing the wealth of monasteries and borrowing money. Already in the 14/15th century, Florence businessman Giovanni Morelli (1371-1444) told his sons, "Avoid falsehoods like the plague – except to escape taxes, because then you are not lying to take someone else's goods but to prevent your own from being unjustly seized."[5]

In the Middle Ages harsh taxes caused many revolts of the people, like the Jacquerie in the Isle-de-France in 1358 and the peasants' revolt led by Wat Tyler against a poll tax in England in 1381. Those revolts were pitilessly put down and their leaders were executed.

More successful tax revolts later by wealthier people helped to change the course of history. In England, property owners protesting against King Charles I's ship tax to raise money for his navy began the Civil War, leading to his execution in 1649. In America in the 1770s, resistance to unfair taxation was one of the causes of the War of Independence.[6] A tax on American, but not British, tea importers had given British importers an unfair

5. Fernand Braudel, *The Wheels of Commerce: Civilisation & Capitalism, 15th-18th Century*, Fontana Paperbacks, 1982, p. 521. 6. The British Currency Act of 1764, prohibiting American colonies from issuing their own currency, was another.

advantage. In Boston on the evening of 16 December 1773, 150 men, pretending to be Mohawk Indians, boarded three British ships, broke open the tea chests, and threw them into the harbour. As news of the 'Boston Tea Party' spread, similar acts of resistance elsewhere led to the War of Independence, which the Americans won. 'No taxation without representation' was confirmed as an important principle of democracy: people should only have to pay taxes agreed by their elected representatives.

That restriction on raising taxes in England had been imposed on the English monarchy by Parliament after the Civil War (1642-1651). It meant that King William III had to get round Parliament to raise money for his wars against France. He did so through setting up the Bank of England in 1694 to lend the money to him. That turned out to be a landmark event in the modern history of money, as described later in this chapter.

Strong hostility to taxation still exists today, and banks and commercial lawyers have evolved arrangements to enable rich and powerful people and businesses to avoid paying their due taxes. But those are now coming to be seen as a major injustice to other citizens, including the citizens and governments of poor countries.[7]

However, it is difficult to achieve international agreement to limit the activities of tax havens. As we shall see in Chapter 4, one of the advantages of a tax reform replacing existing taxes with payments to society for the value of common resources used by people and businesses for their own benefit, is that paying those would be more difficult to avoid.

Trade, paper money, banknotes and 'bankers' tricks'

In the 12th and 13th centuries AD, armies from all over Christian Europe had joined one another in Crusades to capture Jerusalem from the Muslims. One result was increasing trade between those European countries themselves and between Europe and the East.

The growth of trade brought wealth to Italian cities like Venice, Genoa and Florence, situated between the spices and silks of Asia and the markets for them in northern Europe. More trade meant more borrowing by merchants, like Antonio in Shakespeare's *The Merchant of Venice*, to pay the costs of trading until the

7. See, for example, 'Tax Havens Cause Poverty', http://tinyurl.com/ykqodjt.

profits came in. Exchange of currencies also grew – for example by merchants from Italy needing to change profits from sales of Italian wool in France into ducats to spend at home on preparations for future trading expeditions.

As the need for banking and money-changing grew, it became more profitable. The most successful bankers were from Florence.[8] By the 15th century Cosimo de Medici had built up a multinational bank with branches in Avignon, Bruges, London and various Italian cities. He became the ruler of Florence. He and his grandson, Lorenzo the Magnificent, commissioned numerous buildings and works of art by Renaissance masters like Brunelleschi, Botticelli and Michelangelo, and turned Florence into the city we still know today.

Paper money had been used in China for many years. When Marco Polo returned to Venice from China in 1295, he described in *The Travels of Marco Polo* how Kublai Khan's government issued paper money notes authenticated by his officials. Everyone throughout China was compelled to accept them as money, and anyone who counterfeited them was sentenced to death. Being able to create unlimited amounts of paper money gave the Great Khan more scope to encourage economic activity in his country than rulers in Europe who depended on having enough gold and silver to mint coins.

Marco Polo's book encouraged the use of paper in Europe for money dealings. Paper 'bills of exchange' helped merchants and bankers to do business in different places. Instead of carrying heavy loads of coins with him, a merchant could buy a paper bill of exchange from his banker before he set out from home. It would instruct the banker's agent in a foreign city to pay the merchant a certain sum of money in that city's currency at a certain time in the future, so that he could get the money to spend there when he arrived.

Bankers and goldsmiths also gave paper notes as receipts and 'promises to pay' to customers who had deposited coins and gold and silver with them for safekeeping. As time passed, people found it convenient to pay one another by exchanging those bankers' notes. Over the following centuries the notes became a widely accepted substitute for money.

In the 16th century Father Lainez (1512-1565), the General of the Jesuit order of priests who succeeded its founder Ignatius Loyola, said that the merchants and bankers "have so many tricks for inventing ingenious practices that we can hardly see what is going on at the bottom of it all".[9] Earlier the tricks had mostly

---

8. See, for example, Tim Parks' fascinating book, *Medici Money*, Profile Books, 2006.
9. Fernand Braudel, op. cit., page 565 (see footnote on p. 49).

been designed to conceal that the bankers were lending money for interest, which was a sin according to Christian teaching. But, as that teaching relaxed, bankers felt able to profit more openly from lending money for interest and learned a new trick – how to create money out of nothing in order to lend it out at a profit. It is a trick we still suffer from today, costing us billions of pounds, dollars, euros or whatever other established currencies we use.

The bankers had learned that, with their paper banknotes circulating as means of payment, they were seldom asked to pay out more than a fraction of the gold and silver that their customers had deposited with them. So they realised that they could lend out more money in the form of paper banknotes than the value of the precious metals they held. The interest the banks could get from lending paper banknotes was much greater than the cost of printing them, so creating them to lend them was very profitable.

The risk was that, if their customers began to suspect that their bank had issued more notes than it had real money in reserve to back them up, there could be a 'run on the bank'. Its customers would rush to get their money out; and when they found it wasn't there the bank would collapse and many would lose their money altogether. As the use of banknotes as money increased over the years, a run on one bank could affect others, leading to a wider financial collapse with disastrous consequences for many people.

Eventually, by the middle of the 19th century, it was evident that what had originated as credit notes of private banks had become actual money. In Britain, conditions after the Napoleonic wars and as the industrial age developed meant that failure to control the issue of banknotes was damaging the whole economy. The Bank Charter Act of 1844 resulted in giving the Bank of England the monopoly of issuing banknotes in England and Wales, with equivalent controls on the continuing issue of banknotes by commercial banks in Scotland and Ireland. Today the European Central Bank and other central banks also print banknotes on behalf of their governments.

Although the bankers could no longer create money out of nothing in the form of banknotes that people could use *outside* the banking system in payments to other people, they had another trick up their sleeves. They had developed a way to create money out of thin air that their customers could pay one another *inside* the banking system. They created it by simply writing the money into a customer's bank account as a loan ('credit') and then, as instructed by the customer, transferring it as payment into other customers' bank accounts.

For many years that method of creating and circulating money within the banking system was done on paper. But in the past half-century electronic, 'digital' money has steadily replaced paper-based money. That has been accompanied by a shift in the make-up of the total money supply, away from debt-free cash (banknotes and coins) to bank-account money created by the commercial banks as debt – in the UK from 21% cash in 1963 to less than 5% at the end of 2010.[10] Most of the money that most people in 'developed' countries now receive and spend is credited to or debited from our bank accounts without having been converted from or into cash.

In recent centuries, many prominent people have questioned the way banks are allowed to create money, including a number of US Presidents, other government leaders like Napoleon and Bismarck, thinkers like Tolstoy, and others – including leading bankers. For example, Reginald McKenna, Chairman of the Midland Bank, is reported to have said to his shareholders in 1924:

> "I am afraid the ordinary citizen will not like to be told that the banks can and do create money. And they who control the credit of the nation direct the policy of Governments and hold in the hollow of their hand the destiny of the people."

And, speaking to a Texas university audience in 1928, Lord (Josiah) Stamp, a director of the Bank of England, is said to have told it:

> "Banking was conceived in iniquity and was born in sin. The bankers own the earth. Take it away from them, but leave them the power to create money, and with the flick of the pen they will create enough deposits to buy it back again. However, take it away from them, and all the great fortunes like mine will disappear; and they ought to disappear, for this would be a happier and better world to live in. But, if you wish to remain the slaves of bankers and pay the cost of your own slavery, let them continue to create money."

The US Money Masters and the UK Money Reform Party both include those two in the much longer lists of similar quotations on their websites.

The monetary reform needed to deal with that survival from a pre-democratic past is described in Chapter 3.

---

10. I owe that figure to Michael Rowbotham's path-breaking book *The Grip of Death*.

The Bank of England: the first central bank

In 1694 William III of England needed large sums of money for his war against France under Louis XIV. This led to a crucial new development aimed, like so many others in the history of money, at concealing what was actually happening. Following the outcome of the Civil War earlier in the 17th century, William was obliged to persuade Parliament to agree that he could raise higher taxes to finance the war. Parliament was unwilling to agree. So, William Paterson, a Scotsman, arranged for a group of businessmen in the City of London to set up a bank to lend King William the money he needed. As the bank of the King's government it was called the Bank of England, but it remained a privately owned commercial bank until it was nationalised in 1946.

The new Bank of England was able to rely on the government to pay the interest on the loans out of taxes to be raised in future years. As William Paterson advertised it to potential investors, "The bank hath benefit of interest on all moneys which it creates out of nothing." So it was prepared to lend money without insisting that the government should pay it back at any particular time, provided that it continued to pay interest on it. That encouraged the government to borrow more and more. Governments elsewhere in the world have followed suit, and almost every country has built up a growing National Debt. Taxpayers were left out of the decision until after the event; public borrowing and public debt became established as fixtures; and the taxes we have to pay in the UK as annual interest on outstanding public debt in 2011 of over £1 trillion are estimated at £43bn.

A similarly profitable contemporary collaboration for private-sector finance with government, designed to mask the true tax consequences of public spending, was initiated in the UK in 1992. It was called the Private Finance Initiative (PFI). It was started by John Major's Conservative Government and enthusiastically taken up by the following Blair/Brown Labour Government. For technical accounting reasons, the financial commitments under it to pay private sector corporations for financing and managing new schools, hospitals, transport facilities and other public infrastructure projects, have not had to be shown on the government's balance sheet. But the financial commitments of taxpayers for the investment costs and future annual management costs under the scheme were estimated to have grown to a total of £267 billion by November 2010. The government also carries the risk that private sector contractors may be unable to carry out these essential public projects satisfactorily over the next thirty years.

Over the three centuries since it was founded as a bank serving the interests of the king, the Bank of England has evolved step by step into a central monetary authority responsible for serving the public interest. In 1946 it was nationalised and became an agency of the state.[11] In 1997, under the incoming Labour Government, it became independently responsible for achieving monetary objectives publicly laid down and monitored by the elected government and parliament. But for the present, like most other central banks, it still has to let the commercial banks actually create the money supply. It can control only indirectly how much they lend, by raising interest rates if it wants them to create less and lowering them if it wants them to create more.

The disastrous boom and bust of 2007/8 and its continuing consequences suggest a further evolutionary step for the Bank of England. It should take over from commercial banks the actual creation of the bank-account money supply, as it took over the issue of banknotes in 1844. Chapter 3 discusses what this would mean.

About booms and busts

Almost anything can be the subject of boom and bust – like the tulipomania which gripped the citizens of Amsterdam in 1633 and made them drive up the price of tulip bulbs beyond all reason until the price suddenly collapsed, leaving many of them penniless.

Then there was Paterson's Scottish compatriot, John Law. He had killed a man in London in 1694 in a dispute about a woman and money, and was sentenced to death for murder. He escaped and spent years in Scotland, Italy, Holland, Germany and France – gambling, studying banking schemes, and making money. His big opportunity came in Paris in 1715.

The Sun King, Louis XIV, had died leaving huge debts and a chaotic financial situation in France. The Duc d'Orléans had to deal with it as regent for Louis' five-year-old great-grandson Louis XV. The duke agreed that Law should set up a bank that issued its own banknotes. It was so successful that by 1719 Law had become Minister of Finance and his bank, now called

11. Most other central banks now are agencies of the state – the US central bank, the Fed, being the outstanding exception.

'Banque Générale', had taken over the Mississippi settlement of Louisiana in North America and other French overseas trading companies.

Law's 'System' combined issuing money with banking and lending activities, managing the national debt, and controlling much of France's overseas trade. Competing to buy its shares, frenzied Parisians drove their price sky-high. But Law issued so many banknotes and shares that they lost their value, and as people panicked to sell them, the 'Mississippi Bubble' burst. Law's whole System collapsed in 1720; people lost their money; and Law was dismissed. He died in Venice in 1729.

Later in the 18th century Adam Smith described John Law's French venture as "the most extravagant project both of banking and stock-jobbing that, perhaps, the world ever saw"; Voltaire described it as "a stupendous game of chance, played by an unknown man, and a foreigner at that, against a whole nation"; and in the 19th century Karl Marx described Law as having "the pleasant mixed character of swindler and prophet". People in France remembered Law 70 years later when the revolutionary government of 1789 issued so much paper money as 'assignats' that by 1796 they were worth less than the cost of printing them. Later economic historians concluded, rightly or wrongly, that those two unhappy experiences caused French financiers and capitalists to resist the adoption of paper money, which weakened the ability of France to compete with the British industrial economy in the 19th century.

In London the Bank of England was lucky to survive its first few years, having also issued too many banknotes. Then in 1719-20 London experienced the South Sea Bubble. So many people swarmed to buy shares in the fraudulent South Sea Company that they drove up the price a hundred times in a few months. They then all panicked and rushed to sell the shares. So the South Sea Bubble burst in London as the Mississippi Bubble had done in Paris. Many people lost all their money, and the government resigned.

The Mississippi and South Sea Bubbles are examples of the frequent booms and busts in the history of money. A boom tends to start with people increasing their purchases of speculative assets like shares or houses, whose values they expect to rise. As more and more people compete to buy them before their values rise too high, and as more and more bankers compete to create and lend more money to customers to buy them, values continue to spiral higher and higher until they reach a level that seems too high to last.

That starts off the bust. People rush to sell their speculative investments before their values fall further. Many who have borrowed money to buy them now find that selling them won't bring in enough money to repay the debt. Banks and other lenders find that they can't recover the money they have lent. If they have borrowed it from money deposited by their customers, they find they can't repay it. Their customers, getting wind of that possibility, rush to withdraw their deposits from the bank before other customers withdraw it all. That creates a 'run on the bank' as it did to Northern Rock in the UK in 2007, with long queues of customers waiting outside the bank hoping to recover their money.

The biggest boom and bust in the 20th century was the great Wall Street crash of 1929, followed by the worldwide economic depression of the 1930s that led to the Second World War. This is what happened:

- investors frantically bought shares with borrowed money created and lent for that purpose;[12]
- share values rose spectacularly;
- many investors became millionaires on paper;
- they continued to buy shares, assuming that the 'bull market' would continue and eventually allow them to sell their shares at a high enough profit to pay back their loans and keep a profit;
- Irving Fisher, one of the most highly respected American economists of the time, stated confidently on 15 October 1929 that "the nation is marching along a permanently high plateau of prosperity";
- in fact, people were already beginning to have doubts;
- nine days later on 24 October a self-reinforcing 'bear market' set in and prices collapsed, losing $16 billion in value – a huge sum of money in those days;
- bankrupt speculators were said to have jumped to death from skyscraper windows, hundreds of American banks went bust, and thousands of bank customers lost all their money.

12. This is described in bankers' jargon as 'leveraged' investment.

As the money system has been allowed to develop in more and more complicated ways, it has thrown up many new opportunities to make money out of money by more and more complicated forms of betting – on changes in the values of different currencies, for example, and many other forms of what are called 'derivatives'. That was what brought Barings Bank to an untimely and inglorious end in 1995, when one of its traders lost it £860 million by betting on derivatives in Singapore.

Banks gambling with our money on derivatives, and creating new money to lend to other banks in order to trade packages of insecure debts with each other, have helped to cause the particular severity of the present global financial crisis. Many people hoped that it might have culminated in 2007/2008. But by now its consequences are still becoming worse. Sir Mervyn King, Governor of the Bank of England, is reported to have accepted that it might turn into the worst international financial collapse of all time, not excepting the Great Depression of the 1930s. It is becoming clearer and clearer that the simple monetary reform that will be proposed in Chapter 3 must be urgently put into practice.

The Industrial Revolution, Britain's financial supremacy, and opposition to capitalism

The first iron bridge in the world was built over the River Severn in Shropshire by Abraham Darby III in 1779. Abraham Darby I (1678-1717), his grandfather, had discovered how to use coal instead of charcoal to make iron. This led to the use of iron to make engines and machines of every kind, and to build railways and ships and factories. It made the Industrial Revolution possible, and helped Britain to dominate the world's manufacturing, trading and shipping businesses, and to become the most powerful 19th-century nation. The pound sterling became the main international currency, with London becoming the world's financial centre and channelling large sums of money to governments and companies for projects all over the world.

The Darbys were outsiders – Quakers, a sect of non-conformist Protestants still kept out of university and professional and military jobs because of their religion. The enterprising pioneers of the Industrial Age included many other nonconformist outsiders too, like the families of Barclays and Lloyds. They expanded from brewing and ironmongery into providing banking services for other growing businesses. Two hundred and fifty years later, Barclays and Lloyds have become big impersonal multinational banks, established players in the global money game.

Britain's industrial progress benefited from its international trade in two ways. First, trade provided export opportunities, as in the notorious 'trading triangle' between Europe, Africa and America. Ships took textiles, iron, guns and trinkets from Britain to Africa and exchanged them for African slaves; they took the slaves to North and South America and the Caribbean, and sold them to owners of plantations and mines in exchange for sugar, tobacco, gold and silver; and they brought those back to Europe. This profitable three-way trade peaked between 1740 and 1810. It greatly increased the population and prosperity of the port cities of Liverpool and Bristol, and quickened London's development as the world's financial centre. The second way trade helped industrial progress was that it provided investment money. For example, Quaker friends invested profits from the Bristol trade in the Darby ironworks.

The Barings and Rothschilds were also outsiders. They were two families from Germany who came to England, set up banks in the City of London, and eventually became very wealthy and powerful members of the British aristocracy. In 1803, when Napoleon needed money for his wars and offered to sell Louisiana to the USA for $15 million, Barings lent the USA the money to pay him; so Louisiana became part of the USA instead of belonging to France. After Napoleon's defeat in 1815, when Barings raised a loan of 315 million francs for the new French government, the Duc de Richelieu said "There are six Great Powers in Europe: England, France, Prussia, Austria, Russia and Baring Brothers." Barings continued to trade until 1995, when the 'derivatives' trader in Singapore brought it to its end.

Nathan Rothschild set up a bank in London in 1809. His four brothers also had banks – in Frankfurt, Paris, Vienna and Naples. He used the family's network of couriers to supply Wellington's armies with money in the war against Napoleon. They also brought him very useful news. The story is that when Napoleon lost the battle of Waterloo, Nathan heard about it before anyone else at the London stock exchange. He immediately sold all his British government stocks, to trick everyone else into thinking Napoleon must have won and selling their shares too. The price of the shares then fell, and Nathan bought them up cheap. When Wellington's victory became public knowledge Nathan made a fortune. He then became a very successful international

Tax shifts are linked to changes in society

In the 19th century an important shift in taxation was connected with the industrial revolution, with Britain's international supremacy in trading, and with the great parliamentary Reform Act of 1832. The Corn Laws had taxed wheat, barley, rye and oats imported from other countries, making them expensive and restricting the amounts imported. This protection against foreign competition had kept prices and profits high for the benefit of British aristocratic landowners who had ruled the roost. But the new industrialists in the cities now wanted food to cost less, so that they could pay their workers lower wages, reduce business costs, and sell more machines and other industrial goods at home and abroad. The growing urban working population supported them on this, expecting it to increase their prosperity too. The urban industrialists and their workers eventually got their way and the tax was abolished in 1846.

This 'repeal of the Corn Laws' was a historic event, symbolising that Britain had entered the industrial age. It was also a victory for free trade over protectionism, allowing the nation's consumers to buy food more cheaply from abroad instead of benefiting home food producers by keeping prices high. It showed that free trade can be good for some people and bad for others, depending on the circumstances of the time. Today, the effect of imposing free trade on poorer countries, forcing them to accept rich countries' exports while taxing their exports of food and other commodities to the rich countries, has benefited the rich at the expense of the poor.

The shift of taxation that will be proposed in Chapter 4 could be just as historically significant today as the repeal of the Corn Laws was 150 years ago, if not even more significant. It will be a shift of tax away from taxing the rewards people and enterprises get from their contributions to the common wealth and well-being – their earnings from useful work, their profits from useful enterprise, and the value added by their work and enterprise; and a shift of taxes on to charging people and businesses for the value subtracted from the common wealth for their own benefit by the use they are able to make of natural, environmental and publicly created resources. (It will be complementary to changes in how money is created and how public expenditure is spent, as explained in Chapters 3 and 4).

banker. By 1832 he was speaking for the City of London: "This country is the Bank for the world. . . . All transactions in India, in China, in Germany, in the whole world are guided here and settled through this country." Rothschilds later played a big part in the California Gold Rush (1849), in the British Government gaining control of the Suez Canal (1879), and in financing railways around the world.

By the middle of the 19th century the poverty of working people in European cities became so severe that in 1848 the French political philosopher Alexis de Tocqueville (1805-1859) said, "We are sleeping on a volcano. . . . A wind of revolution blows, the storm is on the horizon." In that same year Karl Marx (1818-1883) and Friedrich Engels (1820-1895) published the Communist Manifesto, and revolutions took place in France, Germany, Italy and Austria-Hungary. They were all stamped out. For Karl Marx, this confirmed the lesson of Britain's parliamentary reform in 1832: when the middle-class business owners of capital had achieved their political aims, they would no longer help working people to achieve theirs. His book *Das Kapital* persuaded many people that, under capitalism, money was used to exploit workers in Europe and subject peoples in European colonies. In response to these conditions, trade unions grew up to campaign for better wages for workers; communists ruled Russia for 70 years after the 1917 revolution; and socialist governments have been elected in many other countries since the Second World War. But supporters of the labour interest and socialism have not reformed the money system. How it works and how it could be made to work better is still a mystery to them.

The rise of America and the one-world economy

In the 18th century when Britain ruled its colonial empire, the British government refused to let its American colonists control their own taxes and currency. The resulting dispute provoked the Americans to fight successfully for their independence in 1776. That link between the people being free and having control of their money was basic to their outlook on life.

After independence America grew and developed with astonishing speed. For example, 100 squatters at Chicago in 1830 became 'the first city of the prairies' with more than half a million people in 1880 and a million in 1890. By then, little more than a century after the Declaration of Independence that "all men are created equal", the 'Robber Barons' were creating huge fortunes for themselves with ruthless enterprise, paying rock-bottom wages to thousands of immigrant workers from Europe. One of these tycoons of the railway age was John D. Rockefeller (1839-1937). He set up Standard Oil, became the USA's first billionaire, and gave $500 million to medical research. Another was Andrew Carnegie (1835-1919). He came from Scotland as a boy in 1848 and built up a huge steel industry. Then, saying it was disgraceful if a man died rich, he gave away $400 million, including the cost of 3,000 public libraries in America, Britain, Europe and Africa. A third was the banker John Pierpont Morgan (1837-1913). He bought up half the American railway system and raised $1.4 billion to buy out Carnegie's steel business. People in the streets sang "Morgan, Morgan, the great Financial Gorgon". He symbolised the power of American money.

Between the wars

In the period between the beginning of the First World War (1914-18) and the end of the Second (1939-1945) the USA replaced Britain as the world's financial superpower. It was also a period of unusually severe money disasters.

The Great Crash on the New York stock-market in 1929 might seem the most dramatic. But in Germany in the early 1920s, runaway inflation had meant that money lost its value and became almost worthless. The prices of everything went sky high. People rushed to the shops with wheelbarrows full of almost worthless banknotes to spend all their wages and savings as fast as they could, before their money lost every bit of its value.

This was one cause of the rise of fascism in Europe, led by Hitler in Germany and Mussolini in Italy, which led to the Second World War. But before that it had revived the question of the Gold Standard.

Within a country the Gold Standard had required banks to give gold in exchange for banknotes if their customers asked for it. In trade between countries it had meant that a country receiving payments in the currency of another could require the paying country to give gold in exchange for its currency. When the Gold Standard was dropped in the 1914-18 war, money no longer had to be exchangeable for gold, and that allowed more paper money to be created and put into circulation.

In the 1920s various countries tried to restore the Gold Standard, in order to keep up the value of money and avoid inflation. But that led to less money in circulation, which in turn damped down economic activity and employment. This caused problems no less serious than inflation had done. In Britain, for example, Winston Churchill's decision as Chancellor of the Exchequer in 1925 to restore the Gold Standard caused nationwide pay cuts and a General Strike of all workers. The Gold Standard was suspended again in 1931.[13]

All these problems contributed to worldwide economic crisis and very high unemployment in the 1930s. In America President Roosevelt brought in the 'New Deal'. It invested large sums of government money in projects to create jobs, including big dams, big power stations and many smaller community schemes. John Maynard Keynes (1883-1946) proposed this for Britain and other countries, and Keynesian economics strongly influenced government policies in many countries until the 1970s. But what actually ended the economic slow-down of the 1930s was massive government spending on armaments for the coming war.

Bretton Woods and after

In July 1944 an international conference met at Bretton Woods in the USA to decide how the post-war international money system could avoid repeating the disasters of the inter-war years. It resulted in setting up the International Monetary Fund (IMF) and the World Bank, and much later the World Trade Organisation (WTO). These bodies are controlled by the USA and other rich and powerful countries as organisations separate from the United Nations itself. Keynes argued that a proper international currency was needed, which would not belong to any single nation. The Americans refused. They wanted to be top financial superpower, with the US dollar replacing Britain's pound as the main international currency. Other countries, virtually bankrupted by the war, had to agree.

A link was kept between the world's money and gold until 1971. Exchange rates between other countries' currencies and the US dollar were fixed, and the USA was obliged to meet requests from other countries to give them gold at a price of $35 an ounce in exchange for US dollars which they had earned in international trade. In 1971, however, the USA under President Nixon found it could no longer repay other countries with gold for all the dollars they were now earning, and the remaining link between the world's money and gold was scrapped. National currencies now 'float' against one another

---

13. For more about gold see Chapter 7.

in value; for example, every day pounds, euros, dollars and other currencies can go up or down compared with one another.

In today's huge market for trading national currencies internationally, only a very small proportion of the transactions are connected with real trade between countries in products like oil or coffee or machinery or in services like travel, insurance services, computer and information services, royalties and licence fees and cultural and recreational services. The rest – over 2 trillion US dollars a day – can be understood as a form of betting, with the aim of making profits from buying and selling currencies in exchange for one another. When everyone decides to sell a particular currency its value can collapse, destroying businesses and jobs in the country to which it belongs.

Ever since the US dollar has stopped being linked to gold there has been no limit to how many dollars the USA can create for other countries to use in international trade and investment. Creating money that other people use brings in a profit, as it did for ancient Athens. In recent years it has resulted in other countries paying an estimated $400 billion a year to the USA, preventing poor countries paying off their debts and stifling their development. Today's international money system can be seen as a cause of injustice and poverty, like a game with an unfair scoring system designed and managed by the biggest players so that they always win. See Chapter 5 for more about this.

In recent years some people have thought that other major currencies, like the euro, the Chinese renminbi (or yuan) and perhaps the Russian rouble should share the profit now enjoyed by the US dollar as the world's main international currency. A genuinely international currency belonging to all the world's people would almost certainly be a more efficient and fairer way to meet our international trading and investment needs, as Keynes suggested, but was rejected by the US at Bretton Woods over sixty years ago. In the more democratic and more conserving age ahead of us it will be the right way to serve the interests of the world's people. Again, see Chapter 5.

Small is becoming more beautiful

After the Great War (1914-1918) and especially in the early 1930s at the time of the Great Depression, movements arose in the industrialised countries to revive financial and economic activities at the local level under local control. But they never became an established mainstream part of the money system, and after the Second World War the rise of socialism left them behind as desirable alternatives to capitalism in Britain and other parts of Europe.

However they are now reviving again worldwide,

- partly as a reaction against the long-term trend toward more centralised national and international economic and financial control,
- partly as a response to the present financial and economic crisis that broke in 2007/2008, and
- partly because more people are beginning to understand that greater local control of local economies can have beneficial results for everyone – by reducing the ecological, social and economic overhead costs of remote control by big government, big business and big money.

The need to recognise the local and household money system as a main feature of the new economy is further discussed in Chapter 6.

Conclusion

This Chapter has outlined some prominent features of the historical background to the practical proposals that will be put forward in Chapters 3-6.

The next chapter (Chapter 2), is about the need for a more intelligent way of thinking about how the money system works and how it should work, compared with the understanding that has become conventionally accepted by money experts in recent years. It might be regarded as more 'philosophical' than this chapter.

Both these aspects of the background can help to throw light on the changes we must now make in the way the money system works to meet the challenges facing our one-world society today.

CHAPTER 2

Money and ethics

How money reflects values and embodies them

Money values are values expressed quantitatively. Their numbers in units of pounds, dollars, euros and other currencies show the money value of different activities and things – what we earn, the price of goods and services, the profits made by businesses, and the value of most activities and things involved in the way we now live.[1] These numbers enable us to compare the money values of different activities and different things with one another, as guides to what we should do.

If other things are equal, we will choose to act in ways that tend towards increasing the amount of money we get and reducing the amount of money we spend. In other words, money values encourage most of us to behave in accordance with the Micawber principle:

> "annual income twenty pounds, annual expenditure nineteen pounds nineteen and six, result happiness;
> annual income twenty pounds, annual expenditure twenty pounds ought and six, result misery."[2]

One lesson from history (Chapter 1) is that a main unspoken – and by most people unrecognised – purpose of the money system has been to transfer wealth and well-being to rich and powerful citizens and countries from poorer and weaker ones.

---

1. Although important aspects of many people's lives are still 'unmonetised', money values now motivate the ways of life for most people in almost every part of the world. 2. Mr Micawber was a character in Charles Dickens' 1850 novel *David Copperfield*. A modern equivalent would be "Annual income, £20.00, expenditure £19.95, result happiness; annual income £20.00, expenditure £20.05, result misery."

We now have to recognise the urgent need to redefine the purposes of the money system, in order to meet the threats that face us in the 21st century. As the Introduction suggested, recognising that need – as simple as recognising that the Earth goes round the sun – is the *intellectual* breakthrough on which a *practical* programme for modernising the present money system must be based. We can see it as a 'new Copernican revolution'.

The connection between economists and the money system

Many of today's 'experts' in money and economics find it difficult to accept that defining the purposes of the world's money system is relevant to their professional work. Their attitude was confirmed by the following letter in *The Times* of 8th March 2011, prompted by the news that the London School of Economics had accepted big sums of money from the Libyan government.

> "Sir, Around 1991 I offered the London School of Economics a grant of £1 million to set up a Chair in Business Ethics. John Ashworth, at that time the Director of the LSE, encouraged the idea but he had to write to me to say, regretfully, that the faculty had rejected the offer as it saw no correlation between ethics and economics. Quite." Lord Kalms, House of Lords.

Since March 2011 growing public scandal over the LSE's acceptance of that money has led to the resignation of LSE director, Sir Howard Davies. Former Lord Chief Justice Lord Woolf was asked to conduct an enquiry on what went wrong, his highly critical report has been published, and the acting Director has said that his recommendations will all be implemented. She has said that the LSE "will create an ethics code to cover the entire institution" (*The Times*, 1st December 2011).

A sign of progress, perhaps. But the majority of other academic economists too, especially those financed by big banks and other big businesses, have until recently taught their students: Don't confuse economics with ethics.

When you think about it, that attitude is absurd. It implies that economic understanding is not intended to help anyone to decide to do anything about anything – whether to do one thing rather than another; or to do what you think is good and avoid doing what you think is bad. If economics did have any influence on people's decisions, questions would automatically arise whether its influence is good or bad and whether actions based on its advice tend to be right or wrong. In fact those questions do arise all the time, raising further important ethical questions that the dominant school in the academic economics profession has now been trained to ignore.

In mainly reflecting the interests of the rich and powerful, the unspoken purpose of the money system has also helped to support the self-referential assumption that money's purpose is to make more money. This doesn't only affect how people and businesses conduct their own lives. In recent years the dominating aim of public policy has been the concept of 'economic growth', calculated roughly by the growth of the total amount of money circulating in a country's economy from year to year, but paying little attention to how the money is created and how it is got or spent.

A serious ethical problem arises at present from this reliance of economics on money. In economic analyses of situations requiring supply to be matched with demand, the concept of demand is based on who has enough money to decide to spend it on whatever is to be bought and sold. So in famines, when the actual demand for food is overwhelming, there is no 'economic demand' for it because poor and hungry people have no money.

Ethical questions are, of course, the stuff of politics and political philosophy and political economy. In a comment welcoming a widely acclaimed recent book on Prosperity Without Growth, the distinguished ecological economist Herman Daly contrasts its message with "academic economists' long track-record of mind-numbing irrelevance".[3]

So why is money so important for the discipline of economics, apart from the fact that money finances it just as it finances most other activities? The answer is that money values provide the basic material for what economists are expected to know about.

The *raison d'être* for economists and their knowhow is to work out whether the profits, prices and costs arising from one possible course of action will probably be higher or lower than those of other possible courses. Being concrete numbers indicating the relative prices and costs of everything in comparison with everything else to which prices and costs can be applied, money values are used by economists to calculate their conclusions. On the assumption that the numbers are objectively valid, economists hope to reach scien-

3. Herman Daly's 'Further Commentary' in Tim Jackson, *Prosperity Without Growth: Economics for A Finite Planet*, Earthscan, 2009.

tifically objective conclusions about what the costs and benefits of taking different courses of action would be.

Unfortunately, however, numerical money values have no objective scientific validity. Those numerical values have been generated by a money system that works in ways designed by representatives of the rich and powerful to favour their interests against the interests of the poorer and weaker (as explained in Chapter 1). No wonder that the calculations of economists, too complicated for most citizens to understand, tend to come up – hey presto! – with conclusions that benefit the rich and powerful at the expense of the poor and weak.[4]

As understanding spreads that, being a manmade invention, money does not provide an objective calculus of values beyond human control, and that the money values of different things change in comparison with one another according to changes made in how the money system works, trust in conventional economics as a science will continue to decline. As more and more people realise that the money values existing now have been generated with an ulterior purpose which works against the common human interest, hostility will grow towards the managers of the money system and the economists – not to mention the politicians – who support the way it is now managed. We are obviously not "all in this together".

The stand-off between economics and ethics

The background to today's conventional stand-off between conventional economics and ethics can be traced back to the efforts of leaders of the academic discipline of economics towards the end of the nineteenth century. They were concerned to loosen the link between political economy and the metaphysical approach that was becoming established in academic moral philosophy at that time.

Political economy means the study of the state, the market economy and the citizen; the principles, institutions and practices that connect them with one another; and the forms they may take or the ways they may change at particular times in particular places. In the 21st century it is about the international, national and local systems of laws and money (i.e. the rules and

4. It would be surprising – until you realise who is mainly employing and financing most economists – how few of them tell us how the money system works to generate the money values that it does, and what purposes it works for as a whole.

scoring system, as for a game), and the institutions responsible for deciding how they work – and for managing and enforcing them. Its meaning is illustrated by the following phrases – 'the new political economy of the environment', 'China's new political economy', 'West Africa's changing political economy', 'the very changeable nature of the global political economy', 'the new political economy of welfare', and even 'the political economy of money'.

The academic subject of political economy up to the 19th century had grown out of ethical and moral philosophy, exploring what those political and economic principles should be, and how they should be put into practice. Plato's *Republic* and Aristotle's *Ethics* and *Politics* in Greece in the 5th and 4th centuries BC are early examples. Adam Smith was the Professor of Moral Philosophy in Glasgow and published *The Theory of Moral Sentiments* in 1759 – seven years before he published *The Wealth of Nations* that earned him the title of 'father of economics'.[5] The 19th-century philosopher John Stuart Mill (1806-1873) is best known for his *Principles of Political Economy* (1848). His professed aim, "to unite the greatest individual liberty of action, with a common ownership in the raw material of the globe", combined economic democracy with the end of economic growth. It is more relevant today than ever.

Typical of the development of academic economics toward the end of the 19th century was what was happening at Cambridge University.[6] Professor Alfred Marshall (1842-1924), who led economics at Cambridge, was finding that being under the Moral Sciences Board was putting off potentially good students who wanted to study economics more scientifically than fitted the Board's metaphysical concerns. In 1903 he persuaded the university to set up an independent Economics and Politics department with economics in the lead.

Since then, although outstanding economists like Marshall himself, then John Maynard Keynes (1883-1946) and currently Amartya Sen (1933-) have remained strongly committed to the moral and ethical aspects of economics, the majority of conventional academic economists today have found it easier

---

5. (1) As a moral philosopher, Adam Smith saw the first part of virtue as "the judging faculty, the faculty which determines not only what are the proper means of attaining any end, but also what ends are fit to be pursued, and what *relative value* [my italics] we ought to put upon each. This faculty Plato called, as it is very properly called, reason, and considered it as what had a right to be the governing principle of the whole". (Adam Smith, *The Theory of Moral Sentiments*, Part VII, Section II, Chapter II, p. 316, Cambridge Texts in the History of Philosophy, Cambridge University Press, 2002). (2) James Buchan, *Adam Smith and the pursuit of perfect liberty*, Profile Books, 2006, provides a readable and moving corrective to the simplistic amoral view of many contemporary economists on what Adam Smith meant by "the invisible hand". 6. Robert Skidelsky, *John Maynard Keynes*, Vol. 1, pp. 40-50, Macmillan 1983, gives an interesting account of it.

to get financial support from money-making sources by distancing themselves from ethics. Ironically, many potentially good students now, looking for a field of learning that will enable them do something useful and valuable with their working lives, are put off economics by its pretensions to be an objective science, independent of morality and ethics.[7]

Those pretensions were well illustrated by the hostile responses of conventional economists to two international reform movements – the late 19th-century Georgist movement initiated by Henry George in the USA and the early 20th-century Social Credit movement initiated by C.H. Douglas in Britain. Both those movements campaigned for the ethical purpose of making the money system work for the common interest. The Georgists proposed to do it by a tax shift to Land Value Tax, and the Social Crediters proposed to do it by reforming how the national money supply is created and managed, and combining that with distributing a form of citizen's income. Both movements attracted international support and continue to exist today. But conventional economists still try hard to discredit their ideas, and keep them off mainstream agendas for economic study and public and political discussion and debate.[8]

The distinction between facts and values

The only conventional description of the purposes of money has been that it provides a medium of exchange, a store of value, and a unit of account. That description of the purposes of the money system can be traced back to Plato and Aristotle, who saw money as a measure of value that enabled people to trade and exchange other things.[9] But it describes only the main technical functions offered by money, not the human purposes outside the money system itself for which the worldwide human community should use it.

Because virtually nobody explicitly discusses the wider purposes of the money system as a whole, mainstream thinking about it tends to ignore the distinction between facts and values. The experts aim to understand how the

---

7. However, on the philosophical side of the academic divide too, it is noticeable that highly acclaimed recent books on justice – for example, by John Rawls (*A Theory of Justice*) and Amartya Sen (*The Idea of Justice*) – ignore the effect on justice of how money values work as they do, resulting from how they are created and managed. 8. See Appendix 1 for more on the Georgist and Social Credit movements. 9. Plato and Aristotle also agreed on "the paramount monetary principle – that the nature of money is a fiat of the law, an invention or creation of mankind and society rather than a commodity". Stephen Zarlenga, *The Lost Science of Money*, p. 35, American Monetary Institute.

money system actually works – though not necessarily to pass on their understanding of the facts to a wider public. But they don't try to understand how, as a whole system, it might serve real-life values better than it does now.

That would require them to ask and answer questions about whether and how the money system's present workings should be changed in order to motivate us to live and behave in ways that will achieve those wider purposes. Those are questions about valuing, deciding and acting. The answers will be normative, not descriptive.

For example, it is a historical fact that in Britain in the past hundred years the money value of houses measured by actually existing prices has increased very much more than the money value of most other things, including the rewards in wages and salaries that most people get for their work.[10]

On the other hand, whether the contrast between the higher house-price increases and lower increases in goods and commodities and wages and salaries has been a desirable trend that we should keep going, or an undesirable trend that we should stop and put into reverse, or a trend that does not matter much one way or the other, is not a question to which an objective factual answer can be given. It is a question of judgement, of real-life value, of decision and action, about what we should do. It falls within the sphere of moral and political philosophy and political economy.

David Hume explained this distinction between descriptive and normative meanings in his *Treatise of Human Nature* (1739). It has been summarised as "You can't get an 'ought' from an 'is'." It may be factually correct that particular money values were (and are) attached to particular things at particular times and places. But it cannot be concluded that those values were or are objectively correct or incorrect. In that respect they differ crucially from the way that physical measurements provide factual information that is either correct or not – for instance that the length, height and weight of elephants are almost always bigger than those of mice.

It is a descriptive fact that the different money values of houses and everything else at any particular time will significantly depend on how the people

(continued on page 76)

---

10. To take an extreme example, a particular 5-bedroom house in Chelsea in London was sold for £1,000 in 1910; ninety years later it was worth £4.5 million, an increase of 450,000%. That was nearly 37 times greater than the increase in the price of a basket of basic items like bread and potatoes over the same period. See the review on my website of Fred Harrison: *Boom/Bust: House Prices, Banking and the Depression of 2010*, Shepheard-Walwyn, London, 2005 at http://tinyurl.com/83kbk68.

The fuzziness of real-life values

This illustrates the problem of how to change the way the money system works in order to bring the motivating power of concrete money values into support of, instead of opposition to, people's real-life values that are difficult to define and are often in conflict with one another.

Nouns and adjectives used to describe real-life values include:

- justice;
- fairness;
- compassion;
- human rights;
- generosity;
- perseverance;
- hard work;
- good work;
- efficiency;
- excellence;
- feminine and masculine;
- individual, personal, family and organisational;
- ecological, social and economic;
- mechanistic and organic;
- anthropocentric and Gaian;
- medieval, modern and post-modern;
- pre-industrial, industrial and post-industrial;
- democratic and aristocratic, autocratic, hierarchical, bourgeois, plutocratic, technocratic, and theocratic;
- materialist and idealist;
- spiritual, religious and secular;
- working class, managerial and professional;
- popular and academic;
- capitalist and socialist;
- national and multicultural; and
- charitable, public-service and profit-making.

That list of generally applicable values can be extended almost indefinitely, by applying different newly invented values to various categories of people for particular purposes, such as marketing. An example that I enjoyed in the 1970/80s was the Values and Lifestyles Program of the Stanford Research Institute in California.[11]

The SRI researchers identified three main categories of consumers – those motivated by 'need-driven', 'outer-directed', and 'inner-directed' values. The consumption habits of the need-driven were determined by their need for basics and their lack of money; those of the outer-directed by their need to belong, to emulate the trend-setters, and to be seen as achievers; and those of the inner-directed by their need to express themselves, to experience and participate, and to be socially conscious – for example, by supporting such causes as conservation, environmentalism and ethical consumerism.

A fourth category, 'integrated', was for the "rare people who have it all together. They wield the power of outer-directedness with the sensitivity of inner-directedness". But there were not many of these paragons and they could not be identified empirically. (They must have been splendid people just like you and me, dear reader!)

An important finding of these studies was that a shift was taking place from outer-directed to inner-directed values. Lists of past, present and future symbols of success were used to illustrate what this meant.

Studies like that confirm the difficulty of defining values in their broader real-life sense. For example, identifying inner-directed values by what people treat as symbols of success seems like a contradiction in terms; and the prediction 30 years ago that the human future would be shaped by a shift from outer-directed to inner-directed values now appears very questionable. More people in the world than ever before, whether rich or poor, are now driven by the outer-directed need for money – needed by the rich as a source of luxury and competitive symbolic success, and by millions of poor people to enable themselves and their families to survive and live better lives.[12]

---

11. http://tinyurl.com/2k37l. 12. A fuller summary is in Chapter 6, 'Changing Worldviews, Changing Values' in *Future Work* (page 76) available on my website at http://tinyurl.com/7cgx97p.

in charge of the money system make it work – what is taxed and what is not taxed, what is subsidised and what is not, who creates the money supply in what form, and who because of those facts has more money and who has less than other people. It is also a descriptive fact that we can change existing relativities between the money values of different things by changing the way the money system works. But whether we should do so or not, and if so what changes we should make, are normative questions.

Today's conflict between money values and real-life values

Real-life values are much less concrete than money values – much fuzzier and more difficult to define. They reflect a wide variety of inclinations and preferences about what different people think and feel and do and how we conduct our lives. (See box on page 74)

Nonetheless, widespread serious conflict between current money values and widely accepted real-life values suggests that something has gone amiss in the professional and political management of the money system, and that we should try to put it right.

Compared with the precise definition, numerical concreteness and immediate operational force of money values, real-life values are much less tangible and concrete. It is much more difficult to define the differences between, to take two examples, feminine and masculine values or Christian, Muslim and Jewish values, than the difference in value between what you can buy for £1,000 compared with what you can buy for £100.

We must understand why the clearly defined numerical differences in the money values of different things motivate the daily activities of most of the world's seven billion people more directly and immediately than ecological and social and other real-life values generally do. But that makes it all the more important for us to prevent the money system continuing to work in ways that generate comparative money values that motivate us to compete with one another and destroy the resources of the planet.

When existing money values are widely felt to motivate us to behave in contradiction to widely accepted real-life values, we need to remember that existing money values are not objective facts of life outside human control. Money values primarily result from how the money system works. Having invented and developed the money system, humans have the power to change how it works, if we care enough to mobilise that power and exercise it. In principle, if enough of us decide that the way the money system now works must be changed in order to reduce the conflict between present money values and universal values such as "democracy, the rule of law and human rights",[13] we should be able to do so.

In practice, though, it will be easier to start by tackling more specific and easily definable issues, such as what people get paid for doing work of different kinds. Some people are now paid hugely for work which appears to have little real-life value, contrasting with other people who are paid much less for work that appears to have much more value in human terms.

Thus, in October 2006 – before the bank-created crisis engulfed us – the London Centre for Economic and Business Research reported that about 4,200 staff at banks, law firms, accountancy firms and associated businesses in the City – London's financial district – would each be getting a bonus of over £1 million for that year, totalling £8.8 billion.[14] By contrast, the government department of Education and Skills announced that the salary proposed for "excellent teachers" in inner London for September 2007 would be £43,860. And nurses are paid even less than teachers.

Conventional economists try to persuade us that that kind of disparity between money values and human values is an unavoidable outcome of an objective law of supply and demand. People who work in the City of London, they explain, are in high demand because they bring in high profits to the companies and partnerships they work for; teachers and nurses don't bring in nearly as much profit; and the people with the skills and aptitudes to work as successful money dealers and bankers are limited in number, whereas many more people are able to teach and nurse.

What most economists don't recognise is that the money values that determine the outcomes of demand and supply in any particular situation are not objective outcomes of processes governed by Nature or by God. They are outcomes of how powerful people have made the money system work – in this case, so that banking is a hugely subsidised business and governments allow the banks to hold our societies to ransom.[15] That is something that we can change, if we decide it needs changing. Whether and how we should change

13. ". . . democracy, the rule of law and human rights. These are not 'Western' values; they are universal values of the human spirit" – former UK prime minister Tony Blair in *The Times*, 19 March 2011, p. 27. 14. http://tinyurl.com/6m5ew6n. 15. For how this happens and what should be done about it, see Chapter 3 on Managing the national money supply.

it will be an ethical decision, combining practical understanding of how the money system works with deciding the outcomes we should aim for by changing its present way of working.

To take a different example – house prices again – it is not difficult to understand that the huge disparity between the long-term increases in house-prices, compared with the money values of most other things, is due to the following combination of facts:

- land values are not taxed, but business profits, earnings from work, and value added are all taxed;
- consequently the value of land and the houses on it tends to grow faster than the value of other things;
- that encourages banks to create money to lend to borrowers to buy houses and the land they are on; and
- that helps to power the long-term self-reinforcing spiral of rising land values and the values of houses.[16]

Ethical alternatives

The conflict between money values and human values today is largely due to the fact that today's money values reflect purposes of the money system that are now out of date:

- to transfer money, wealth, power and well-being from poor people, organisations and countries to rich ones; and
- to encourage the extraction and exploitation of natural resources.

Until that root cause of the conflict is removed, more people will continue to try to reduce the damaging social and ecological effects of using money in accordance with the existing money values, by using our own money to support ethical alternatives. Those include fair trade, ethical consumption, ethical investment, ethical business practices and other ways of using money ethically.

In *spending* our money, we will not just be trying to buy things as cheaply as possible, but to be ethical consumers – for example to buy energy-saving refrigerators and freezers and other household goods, or 'fair trade' products like coffee imported at fair prices from poor producers in poor countries. In *saving and investing* our money, too, we will not just be trying to make more money but,

16. See footnote 11 on p. 75, and for what should be done about it see Chapter 3 on Managing the national money supply and Chapter 4 on Public revenue and spending.

for example, to invest in enterprises that treat their workers well, help to conserve the environment, or provide goods and services that contribute in other ways to the health and well-being of their customers and the environment. In deciding how we *earn* our money, we will not just be looking for jobs well enough paid to enable us to meet our own and our families' needs and aspirations, but also ones that enable us to do good work useful to other people.

As well as individual people and households, increasing numbers of businesses are becoming seriously involved in 'business ethics' and 'corporate social and environmental responsibility' – not just aiming to make profits, but also to contribute to the well-being of people and the natural environment.

Leading organisations helping them include Jonathon Porritt's and Sara Parkin's Forum for the Future in the UK, working with "leaders from business and the public sector to create a green, fair and prosperous world"; Hazel Henderson's Ethical Markets – and her book *Ethical Markets: Growing the Green Economy* (2007) – and linked initiatives in the US; and The Natural Step (internationally based) that "has helped hundreds of different organisations around the world to integrate sustainable development into their strategic planning and create long-lasting transformative change".

Meanwhile academic interest in business ethics has been developing in enlightened universities, as under Laszlo Zsolnai in Budapest[17] and Peter Reason and his colleagues at Bath University, 1997-2010.[18]

Unfortunately this ethical approach is still virtually unknown territory to those who manage big money – the big banks and other big financial companies. Their objectives are still focused more or less exclusively on making money out of money. They profit from helping their rich customers to reduce the taxes they should pay, they handle money for customers engaged in all kinds of activity, regardless of whether they are ethical or not[19], and they continue to invest far more money in environmentally damaging projects than in environmentally benign ones.[20]

Meanwhile, ethical financial enterprises have been growing fast in the UK in recent years, including the Co-operative Bank. Two others are Triodos Bank and Rathbone Greenbank.

---

17. See http://laszlo-zsolnai.net. Also see the UK Institute of Business Ethics – www.ibe.org.uk. 18. See www.jamesrobertson.com/news-jul11.htm#books; and http://tinyurl.com/6gqaxb9. 19. Questionable ones include former heads of foreign states and their families. 20. For example the Royal Bank of Scotland, now owned by the UK government, "over-invests in fossil fuels and under-invests in renewables and other clean technologies". See http://tinyurl.com/82mwwby.

For those who can afford it, supporting special ethical uses of money, corporate social responsibility and business ethics makes a valuable contribution to a better future. It helps deserving people and businesses, spreads awareness that ethical uses of money are possible, and commits good people to good causes.

But we should recognise that these special uses of money are what environmental engineers call 'end of the pipe' responses to the real problem[21] – the upstream cause of the problem in this case being how the unreformed mainstream money system works.[22] By definition, special ethical uses of money mean swimming against the direction of the prevailing financial flow, whereas what is really needed is to change the direction of the prevailing flow. Until that happens, swimming against it will not be a practical option for most of the world's people, who have to use all the money they can get to meet their personal and family responsibilities and needs.

To bring money values into closer harmony with the universal values of the human spirit we will have to tackle the problem at its roots and reform how the money system works as a whole. That will be the only way to reduce the threat to the future of our species from the systemic ecological destruction, economic inefficiency, and social injustice arising from the way the money system now works.

Religious faiths, ethics and money[23]

We rightly admire people whose faith has inspired them to devote energy and courage, now and in the past, to promoting social and economic justice. Helping to get changes made in an unjust money system is one way of doing that.

But we know too that the faiths have continually used their energy to fight and persecute one another; and even in times of mutual goodwill they have failed like everyone else to secure lasting ethical improvements in the workings of the money system.

---

21. "Methods used to remove already formed contaminants from a stream of air, water, waste, product or similar. These techniques are called 'end-of-pipe' as they are normally implemented as a last stage of a process before the stream is disposed of or delivered." See http://tinyurl.com/7kyuygy. 22. A detached view might also see them as one example of the 'epicycles piled on epicycles' responses to failures in our present 'pre-Copernican' mainstream money system to function in ways we need it to function (see footnote on page 32). 23. My personal views on this subject have not changed much since I led the new economics foundation project on 'Economic Teachings of World Faiths' (1987-1994) – see http://tinyurl.com/7fdnujy on my website.

A historical sketch

Aristotle (384-322 BC), whose thinking in ancient Athens inspired Christian theologians 1,500 years later, held that the natural and proper purpose of money is to enable us to exchange necessities of life, such as items of clothing and food. Our need for most things is limited; we can't wear unlimited clothes or eat unlimited food. But, because money can buy all sorts of different things, some people want unlimited amounts of money, as Midas wanted to turn everything he touched into gold. So people may be tempted to practise usury – to make money out of money by lending it at interest. Aristotle held that that was misguided and wrong.

Jesus (1st century AD) drove the money-changers out of the Temple in Jerusalem for polluting it with their haggling. St Aquinas (1225-1274) and other medieval Christian schoolmen and church leaders taught that the use of money must be controlled by the ethics of right and wrong – by what was a just wage for a particular worker or trader and what was a just price for a particular thing. That teaching meant that lending money at interest was a sin. In the *Inferno*, Dante (1265-1321) described money-lenders wailing in the lowest parts of Hell in their after-life. God had created Nature's resources and human work as the two true sources of wealth, and He had also created time. It was a sin against God for money-lenders to lend money for interest at all, and especially at rates depending on how much time the loan was for.

However, that did not prevent the Medici family from setting up their bank in Florence in 1397. Before its collapse in 1494 the bank had developed into the then equivalent of today's multinational banks. After the Medici bank collapsed, the family were able to use the combined power of money, politics and religion – Popes Leo X and Clement VII were both Medici family members – to influence European events up to the 18th century.

Christian teaching about money changed after the Middle Ages, following the growth of commerce and trade in Northern Europe where the Protestant Reformation against the Catholic Church was strongest. In Germany Martin Luther (1483-1546) preached that useful work in the business of the world was more acceptable to God than the comfortable, escapist life of monks in monasteries. John Calvin (1509-1564), living among the merchants and townspeople of Geneva, taught that the medieval scholastics were wrong, that condemning usury was out of date, that lending money to support business and trade was fulfilling a productive purpose, and that charging someone for borrowing your money was no worse than charging them for renting your house.

Later Protestants went further, teaching that making money out of money was not only permissible; it reflected a positive service to God. If you did not make money when you could, you would be rejecting God's gifts and failing to use them as his steward, as in St Luke's parable of the talents. In due course this turned into the message of capitalism – that making money is a central purpose of human life. It became particularly influential in Britain and America, and now affects people in every part of the world.

When Adam Smith said, "It is not from the benevolence of the butcher, the brewer or the baker that we expect our dinner, but from their regard to their own self-interest", and linked that with the idea that the "invisible hand" of the market will match supply with demand, he meant that, because they have to make money, producers will produce for sale what consumers will pay for.[24]

That is true of markets based on money, of course. In economics, 'demand' depends on the money people have to spend on cheaper or more expensive goods and services, and whether they have the necessary money to spend to meet their needs. In present circumstances markets based on money do not always match supply with everyone's needs. As mentioned earlier, in famines the human demand for food is very high but the economic 'demand' is virtually non-existent because poor and hungry people have no money.

Some contemporary examples of faith concerns

There are many examples of religious concern with economic and financial life today, but comparatively few are explicitly concerned with how the money system now works and needs to be changed.

Strict Islamic teaching is one. It still forbids lending money for interest, seeing it as unjust that a lender of money for a project – say, a new shop – doesn't have to do anything else to make the shop a success while the borrower has to bear all the costs if it should fail. Tarek El Diwany's impressive book[25] ends as follows. "We must somehow overturn the monetary system as

---

24. Adam Smith was arguing for economic freedom against the 'mercantilism' of royalist control of the economy which favoured powerful interests in support of Britain's trading and military power in competition against other nations. He would never have dreamed of saying that making money should be a central purpose of our lives. 25. See Tarek El Diwany, *The Problem With Interest*, Kreatoc Ltd, 3rd edition, 2010. http://tinyurl.com/7lm9mbg.

it is. We need a payment transmission system, a safekeeping service, and investment advisory services. To all these things, yes. To money creation for the sake of profit, no."

Examples of Christian concern with the money system include:

- St Paul's Institute (the director, Canon Giles Fraser, resigned from the Cathedral in late October, 2011 in response to how the Cathedral management proposed to deal with the Occupy London demonstrators outside its doors).[26]
- Social Justice Ireland (Fr Sean Healy and Sr Brigid Reynolds).[27]
- The Christian Council for Monetary Justice (chairman, Canon Peter Challen).[28]
- The Ecumenical Council for Corporate Responsibility.[29]
- Ekklesia – beliefs and values think-tank on religion, politics, theology, culture and society (Jonathan Bartley).[30]

There is also the series of Papal Encyclicals that deal with questions of economic and social justice. The latest of these is Pope Benedict XVI's *Caritas in Veritate* [Charity in Truth], 29 June 2009.[31] It is based on the following principle:

> "*Caritas in Veritate* is the principle around which the Church's social doctrine turns, a principle that takes on practical form in the criteria that govern moral action. I would like to consider two of these in particular, of special relevance to the commitment to development in an increasingly globalized society: *justice and the common good*. . . .
>
> *Charity goes beyond justice*, . . . but it never lacks justice. . . . I cannot 'give' what is mine to the other, without first giving him what pertains to him in justice. . . . .
>
> Besides the good of the individual, there is a good that is linked to living in society: the common good. It is the good of 'all of us', made up of individuals, families and intermediate groups who together constitute society. It is a good that is sought not for its own sake, but for the people who belong to the social community and who can only really

26. www.stpaulsinstitute.org.uk, also see the note on banks' morality at http://tinyurl.com/7crjkad and http://tinyurl.com/7lubxhm. 27. www.socialjustice.ie (includes banking, basic income, taxation and other financial policy issues). 28. www.ccmj.org. 29. See the EECR report of March 2011 on 'The Banks and Society: Rebuilding Trust – social, ethical and environmental concerns', http://tinyurl.com/88vsujo. 30. www.ekklesia.co.uk. 31 http://tinyurl.com/nhvska.

and effectively pursue their good within it. To desire the *common good* and strive towards it *is a requirement of justice and charity*."

However, the encyclical does not deal directly with how money affects justice and the common good. Perhaps the Vatican still recalls the Vatican Bank scandal of 1982 as a topic to be avoided.[32]

Indeed, the organised faiths have not always handled money blamelessly. The sale of pardons by the Catholic Church in the late middle ages shocked Martin Luther and helped to provoke the Protestant Reformation. And today the Church of England has to be urged to use money ethically.[33]

The role of the faiths in global money system reform

In spite of exceptions like Liberation Theology, there is a general worldwide tendency for the faiths to concentrate mainly on preaching individual personal salvation and spirituality to their flocks. Some, such as Buddhism or Christianity, teach that this world is a delusion from which we must detach ourselves or a 'vale of sin' from which we must pass to eternal life in the different world of heaven. Those ideas are likely to weaken most people's commitment to reforming the institutions of money and politics, although reforming them should result in reducing their present pressures on us to sin against one another and the rest of creation.

A possible answer to that is a *both/and* approach, aiming to bring about both the development of ourselves as persons-in-community and changes for the better in the institutions and values of society. That will avoid sterile argument between:

- preachers who say that we must stop being selfish and sinful; we must simply learn to love God, one another and His whole creation, and to treat money accordingly; and
- teachers who say that we must simply learn that you can't change human nature by preaching virtue against sin, and virtuous uses of money against sinful ones.

The more balanced approach recognises that, while human nature necessarily relies on a degree of selfishness to survive and prosper, we also have great

32. See BBC News report at http://tinyurl.com/39m8kxw. 33. See 'Responsible finance and economic justice', 24 Nov 2011 at http://tinyurl.com/7sqkbe2.

potential for altruism. By changing how our institutional structures like the money system now work, we can motivate ourselves to act in ways that serve both our common interests and our own personal interests and responsibilities.

So we need to reconcile money values with real-life values.

New purposes for the money system

So what purposes should guide the development of the world's money system in the 21st century?

As mentioned earlier in this chapter, the conventional description of the purposes of money is that it provides a medium of exchange, a store of value, and a unit of account. But that only describes the main functions of money; it does not suggest what purposes we should use the money system for.

People around the world now share many more common interests than our predecessors in past centuries. We have also developed a single interconnected money system that, by motivating our decisions to a greater or lesser extent, helps to shape the lives of us all. We can no longer ignore the common purposes that we need the money system to achieve for us. We can no longer let it automatically create conflict between money values and real-life values. We must deliberately and intelligently turn it into a source of motivation for ourselves to support the survival and well-being of our species and life on Earth, while at the same time meeting our own needs and those of our families, friends and neighbours.

That will require a new understanding of how the money system works. The key points are that:

- how governments manage their own financial operations on behalf of society largely determines how the money system works as a whole;
- how the money system works shows the money values of everything compare with the money values of everything else;
- those comparative values motivate us to behave and live our lives in some ways rather than others; and
- at present they motivate us to live perversely – not co-operatively but competitively against other people, and not conservingly but destructively of the planetary resources on which the future of ourselves and other life on Earth depends.

How the money system works – a summary
How governments manage their own financial operations on behalf of society largely determines how the money system works as a whole.
How the money system works determines how the money values of everything compare with the money values of everything else.
Those comparative values motivate us to behave and live our lives in some ways rather than others.
At present they motivate us to live perversely – not co-operatively but competitively against other people, and not conservingly but destructively of the planetary resources on which the future of ourselves and other life on Earth depends.

As more citizens of democratic societies in an increasingly democratic and conserving world learn that the money values generated by how the money system works have been continually changed through the centuries to serve the interests of the people in charge of it (as evidenced in Chapter 1), fewer of us will accept it as an objective calculus of values mysteriously gifted to us from on high. We will insist on it being managed on behalf of us all.

That will start us thinking about new purposes and principles for the world's money system on the following lines.

(1) Its purposes should be to:

- enable everyone to benefit more fairly from the activities of producing and exchanging goods and services without over-exploiting the resources of the planet, and
- motivate us and all the world's people to live and organise our lives in ways that enable us to meet the needs of ourselves and our families, friends and neighbours while maintaining the planet's resources to support the survival and well-being of our species and life on Earth.

New purposes for the money system – a summary
To enable everyone to benefit more fairly from the activities of producing and exchanging goods and services without over-exploitation of the resources of the planet.
To motivate us and all the world's people to live and organise our lives in ways that enable us to meet the needs of ourselves and our families, friends and neighbours while maintaining the planet's resources to support the survival and well-being of our species and life on Earth.

(2) It should be organised and managed on the following principles, at national and international levels and – when locally supported – at more local levels too:

- public agencies serving the common interest should create the public money supply;
- people and businesses and other organisations should be rewarded untaxed for the contributions we make by our efforts and skills to the well-being of other people and for the value we add to the value of common resources;
- people and businesses and other organisations, including public service and other non-profit organisations, should be taxed on the value they take from common resources for their own purposes;
- the revenue from those taxes – after democratic decisions on what is needed to finance other public services – should be fairly shared among us all as a Citizen's Income;
- those arrangements should be designed to enable us to meet our own needs in ways that will help others to meet theirs and to conserve our common inheritance of world resources; and finally
- they should free us from continually increasing dependence on centralised national and international money, and on big business and government to meet all our needs, and so enable us to reduce our use of conventional mainstream money.

New principles for the money system – a summary
Public agencies serving the common interest should create the public money supply.
People and businesses and other organisations should be rewarded untaxed for the contributions we make by our efforts and skills to the well-being of other people and for the value we add to the value of common resources.
People and businesses and other organisations, including public service and other non-profit organisations, should be taxed on the value they take from common resources.
The revenue from those taxes – after democratic decisions on what is needed to finance other public services – should be fairly shared among us all as a citizen's income.
Those arrangements should be designed to help us to meet our own needs in ways that help others to meet theirs and to conserve our common inheritance of world resources.
They should free us from continually increasing dependence on centralised national and international money, and on big business and government to meet all our needs, and so enable us to reduce our use of conventional mainstream money.

That last point is crucial. Conventional economic assumptions demand continuing growth of the ecological, social, and financial costs of big government, big business and big money. Those include the costs of:

- expanding and modernising transport and traffic by road, rail, air and sea;
- the continuing expansion and duplication of infrastructures, buildings and services – such as the provision of energy and other resources – to support remotely managed manufacturing, trading and employment; and
- growing administrative, financial, legal and regulatory superstructures.

As the majority of the world follows the Western minority further along the conventional path of development, a clearer view of the future will call into question today's assumptions about money in the economy. For example:[34]

- ***Economic growth*** – How can the volume of worldwide economic activity, measured by the total value of money circulating through the economy, grow *ad infinitum*? Why should it grow *ad infinitum*? Who will benefit from ever greater consumption of the planet's resources, accompanied by ever greater exchanges of money, apart from bankers and other money-system managers?[35]
- ***Full employment*** – Does it make sense to manage the money system to drive as many of us as possible into paid jobs working for other people and organisations richer and more powerful than ourselves? Might it not make better sense if the money system were managed to allow and enable more of us who wish to work, paid or unpaid, for ourselves and one another, on useful and valuable 'ownwork',[36] to do so?
- ***International trade*** – Will it continue to make sense to assume that the total value of international trade should be as high as possible? Why is it beneficial to maximise the money value of countries' exports and imports to and from one another? What is so good about increasing the dependence of countries on one another, and the environmental and financial costs that come with maximising trade?
- ***National and international money supplies*** – Would the common interest be better served at national and global levels by making public agencies

34. It naturally happens that these questions reflect aspects of the sane, humane, ecological (SHE) future discussed in my earlier books since *The Sane Alterative* in 1978. See www.jamesrobertson.com/books.htm. 35. Tim Jackson, in his acclaimed book *Prosperity Without Growth: Economics for A Finite Planet*, makes a compelling case against endless economic growth. Also see footnote 3 on p. 69. 36. www.jamesrobertson.com/books.htm#futurework.

responsible for creating the supplies of money used by people in their different nations and for international purposes? Why do we have to depend as now on giving profit-making commercial banks the double privilege of creating money as debt that pays interest to them, and putting it into circulation in the form of bank loans to their customers for purposes approved by the banks themselves?

- ***The right things to tax*** – Might it be a good idea to consider removing taxes from the rewards (*pay* and *profits*) that people and enterprises earn for *adding value* for society, and replacing them with taxes on the value which, as people or organisations, they *subtract* for their own benefit from the value of public assets and common resources?

Questions about the key assumptions of today's conventional amoral thinking about money – a summary	
Economic growth	How can the volume of worldwide economic activity, measured by the total value of money circulating through the economy, possibly grow *ad infinitum*? Why should it grow *ad infinitum*? Who will benefit from ever greater consumption of the planet's resources, accompanied by ever greater exchanges of money, apart from bankers and other money-system managers – for as long as it lasts?
Full employment	Does it make sense to manage the money system to drive as many of us as possible into paid jobs working for other people and organisations richer and more powerful than ourselves? Might it not make better sense if the money system were managed to allow and enable more of us who wish to work, paid or unpaid, for ourselves and one another, on useful and valuable 'ownwork', to do so?
International trade	Will it continue to make much sense to assume that people in different countries should become ever more dependent on one another, in order to make the total money value of international trade as high as possible?
National and international money supplies	Would not the common interest be better served by making public agencies responsible for creating national and international money supplies instead of continuing to give this privilege to profit-making commercial banks?
The right things to tax	Why not consider removing taxes from the rewards (pay and profits) that people and enterprises earn for adding value for society, and replacing them with taxes on the value that people and enterprises subtract from public assets and common resources for their own benefit?

Two final thoughts – from Keynes

It is fitting to end this chapter with the following thoughts from John Maynard Keynes.

> "When the accumulation of wealth is no longer of high social importance, there will be great changes in the code of morals. We shall be able to rid ourselves of many of the pseudo-moral principles which have hag-ridden us for two hundred years, by which we have exalted some of the most distasteful of human qualities into the position of the highest virtues. We shall be able to afford to dare to assess the money-motive at its true value. The love of money as a possession — as distinguished from the love of money as a means to the enjoyments and realities of life — will be recognised for what it is, a somewhat disgusting morbidity, one of those semi-criminal, semi-pathological propensities which one hands over with a shudder to the specialists in mental disease . . . But beware! The time for all this is not yet. For at least another hundred years we must pretend to ourselves and to everyone that fair is foul and foul is fair; for foul is useful and fair is not. Avarice and usury and precaution must be our gods for a little longer still. For only they can lead us out of the tunnel of economic necessity into daylight." *Economic Possibilities for our Grandchildren* (1930).

> "If economists could manage to get themselves thought of as humble, competent people on a level with dentists, that would be splendid." *The Future – Essays in Persuasion* (1931).

We are now getting on towards the hundred years since Keynes wrote those words. But beware! We are now running out of time. "Avarice and usury" are carrying us all too fast toward self-destruction. Can we wean ourselves off them in time to survive their consequences? That is an open question now.

This brings us to the end of Part 1. The chapters that follow in Part 2 will summarise proposals for the urgently needed practical reforms of the money system. They will take account of the historical lessons from its past in Chapter 1, and the new purposes for its future suggested by this chapter's more philosophical approach.

PART TWO

Proposed reforms

Introduction

The practical proposals in this Part build on the lessons from history and the reflections on money values and ethical values in Part One.

Because the world's money system is now more fully developed at national than at local and international levels, the national reforms proposed in Chapters 3 and 4 provide a model and a context for the international and local proposals in Chapters 5 and 6.

The national reforms proposed here are based on the need for changes in the system now malfunctioning in Britain, but the underlying principles will be common to all countries. Readers in other countries should adapt them to deal with differences there – as in the United States, for example, where their central bank has not yet been fully nationalised.

The central role of governments in the money system

The way governments and government agencies now carry out their central responsibility for how their money systems work must be modernised and comprehensively transformed. That does not mean more privatising of the money system – rather the reverse.[1]

Governments and government agencies should not only continue to be primarily responsible for how public money systems – national and international – serve the common interest. The responsible people in government must carry out that responsibility in a way that makes how they do it much

1. For further discussion see F. A. Hayek *Denationalisation of Money*, http://tinyurl.com/722aqgd, and comments by Huber and Robertson in *Creating New Money*, pp. 50-52. See www.jamesrobertson.com/books.htm#creating.

clearer and easier to understand than it is at present. They must be fully and clearly accountable through democratic procedures that citizens can trust.[2]

National governments and governmental agencies are at present responsible for managing five main money functions.

The first three are the primary ones:

- how the national *money supply* is created (by whom and in what form – either by public agencies debt-free or by commercial banks as profit-making debt);
- how *public revenue* is collected to be spent on public purposes (for example, what is taxed and what is not taxed); and
- what *public spending* is spent on and what it is not spent on.

Those three primary functions are accompanied by two further ones, acting as correctives to problems arising from inadequacies in the first three:

- how money is *borrowed* for public purposes; and
- how the financial activities of individual people and private sector organisations are *regulated*.

In the UK, all five of those functions are carried out under the control of the Treasury. How those governmental functions are carried out has a dominating effect:

- on the flows of money through the economy,
- on the money values and relative prices of almost all our activities and everything we buy and sell, and
- therefore on how the money system motivates us to organise and live our lives, and on the impacts we make on other people and the ecological resources on which we all depend.

Who creates the *money supply* and in what form – as interest-paying debt or free of debt – strongly skews the initial money flows in favour of some activities against others; and the initial effect of that on prevailing money values tends to

---

2. We all need outside reinforcement to resist opportunities for diverting money to ourselves, whether we are working for the public interest or for private profit. It is true that, even in 'highly developed' countries like the USA and UK, activities now take place among public servants – officials, elected representatives, etc. – that can be interpreted ethically, if not legally, as financial corruption. But, in principle, it will always be easier to establish ways that "lead us not into temptation" and guard us against 'moral hazard', if we are working for the common interest rather than for personal or private-sector profit.

persist as the money continues to circulate through the economy as a whole.

Taxes now take more than a third of the value of total economic activity away from some activities, and *public spending* then puts it back into others. Taxes add to the costs of what they tax, while public spending reduces the costs of what it supports. That means that what is taxed and what is not taxed, combined with what public money is spent on and what it is not spent on, powerfully influence how prevailing money values favour certain activities against others right through the economy.

The outcomes of those three functions determine the importance of the fourth and the fifth:

(a) how much money a government has to *borrow*, from whom and at what cost, to remedy its failure to match what it spends with what it is able to raise from taxes; and
(b) how much complex and costly *regulation* of private sector financial activities a government has to set up over and above normal consumer protection laws, owing to failures in how it manages its first three functions.

In other words, the scale of the fourth and fifth functions entirely depends on the size and nature of the undesirable, unintended consequences of design failures in the first three – providing the money supply, raising public revenue, and spending public money. How much a government needs to borrow and how it needs to regulate private sector financial activities is determined by how much it needs to compensate for the effects of failings in those three more basic functions.

Two key consequences

So there are two key consequences of how governments carry out their central role in the money system.

First, the effects of how money is created, how public revenue is raised, and what public spending is spent on, combine to shape the way governments organise and set in motion the flows of money for which they themselves are directly responsible. That then combines with other factors, such as the prevailing supply and demand for some things compared with others, to motivate people and organisations to earn and spend their own money in some ways rather than others.

So the idea that the money system could ever deliver anything resembling a level playing field is sheer fantasy. And that means that democratic governments and government agencies must take positive responsibility for designing, organising and managing the overall money flows in their societies by the ways they handle their own money operations. That must be done in ways that provide people and businesses and countries with incentives to deal with *our own* money in ways that, while serving our own interests, will automatically serve our common ecological, social and economic purposes too.

Second, because the required scale of governments' fourth and fifth financial functions (government borrowing and regulation of private sector financial activities) depends on the scale and nature of failings in the first three (providing the money supply, raising public revenue, and spending public money), the need for the fourth and fifth should be reduced, or even altogether removed, by effective reform of the first three to meet 21st-century purposes.

New purposes and principles

Previous chapters have shown that the world's money system needs new purposes and principles.

Chapter 2 has suggested that a main purpose must be to motivate us all to live in ways that will secure the survival and well-being of our species and life on Earth; and that we must reform the way the money system works so that it will motivate us to do that, instead of motivating us as it does at present.

It has also suggested that the new principles should include organising and managing the money system at every level with that purpose in mind, so that:

- everyone will be free to benefit from fairer, more efficient and more conserving ways of producing and exchanging goods and services;
- people and businesses will be rewarded untaxed for the value we contribute by meeting common needs and conserving common resources;
- in place of taxes on earnings from activities of that kind we will be taxed on the use we make – and so on the value we subtract – from common resources for the private benefit of ourselves and our families, friends and associates;
- the revenue raised by taxing the value we take from common resources will be shared by everyone as a Citizen's Income;

- those arrangements will motivate us to meet our own needs and responsibilities in ways that will help others to meet theirs; and
- they will free us from national and global financial pressures that now limit many people's freedom to live good lives of their own choosing in their own local and household economies.[3]

Necessary reforms in governments' money functions

As it turns out, the effects of how all governments' main money functions are carried out today directly conflict with the outcomes listed above. The next four chapters propose a reformed approach as follows.

Chapter 3. *The national money supply.*
Transfer the function of creating the national money supply *away from* commercial banks as a source of private profit to themselves, *to* the central bank as a source of public revenue to be spent into circulation by the government for public purposes.[4]

Chapter 4. *National public revenue and public spending.*
(1) Shift revenue collection (taxes) *away from* incomes, profits, value added and other financial rewards for useful work and enterprise, and put taxes *on to* value subtracted from common resources such as land and the environment's capacity to absorb pollution and waste (such as carbon emissions); and *prevent tax avoidance* by rich people and businesses using tax havens, etc.[5]

(2) Shift the balance of public spending *away from* perverse subsidies and *from* dependency-reinforcing welfare services provided directly by big government itself or by expensive contracts to big business and big finance, *on to* the distribution of a Citizen's Income directly to all citizens – as their share in the value of common resources which they can use in support of their own well-being.[6]

---

3. See *Future Work* (1985) – www.jamesrobertson.com/books.htm#futurework. This is relevant to Prime Minister David Cameron's hopes for a 'Big Society'. 4. Sources for monetary reform include www.bankofenglandact.co.uk, www.positivemoney.org.uk, www.jamesrobertson.com/links.htm#monetary and www.jamesrobertson.com/books.htm#creating.
5. Sources for the future of taxes include www.taxjustice.net and http://tinyurl.com/7hj7n7c.
6. Sources for future public spending include www.jamesrobertson.com/article/citizensincome.pdf, Norman Myers and Jennifer Kent, *Perverse Subsidies*, Island Press, 2001.

Chapter 5. *The international money system.*
Broadly following the models proposed in Chapters 3 and 4, a new international currency will be proposed, in which a genuinely international money supply will be created to support international trade, operating in parallel with existing national currencies and currencies like the euro; and that will be accompanied with effective arrangements for international public revenue collection and international public spending.

Chapter 6. *The local money system.*
Allow local citizens greater democratic freedom to develop local currencies and other local financial institutions as a basis for more self-reliant local economies.

Chapter 7 will then conclude Part 2 with some further reflections, before the book's Conclusion.

Necessary reforms in governments' money functions – a summary	
National money supply	Transfer the creation of the national money supply away from commercial banks and to the central bank as a source of public revenue.
National public revenue & spending	Shift taxation away from incomes, profits and other rewards for useful work and enterprise, and on to the value subtracted from common resources (e.g. land) and the environment's capacity to absorb pollution and waste.
	Prevent tax avoidance.
	Shift the balance of public spending away from perverse subsidies and dependency-reinforcing welfare services to the distribution of a Citizen's Income directly to all citizens as their share in the value of common resources.
International money system	Introduce new arrangements for international money supply, public revenue and public spending.
Local money system	Improve the self-reliance of local economies by allowing the development of local currencies and other local financial institutions.

CHAPTER 3

Managing the national money supply

Start with the right questions

Impartial visitors from another planet would stand aghast at how we create and manage our national money supply. You can imagine them saying to one another: "These people must be absolutely crazy!" To us they might say, more tactfully, "We wouldn't start from here, if we were you."

We must start by asking the right questions. They include questions about facts and questions about what should be done.

The important factual questions are:

- who creates the money supply and puts it into circulation?
- in what form do they create it: as debt, or free of debt?
- who gets first use of it?
- for what purposes?

The important practical questions are:

- who *should* create it and put it into circulation?
- in what form *should they create it*, as debt, or free of debt?
- who *should* get first use of it?
- for what purposes?

If the way we now manage our national money supply had not grown up bit by bit, century by century; if it had not become thoughtlessly accepted as the status quo; and if we were now starting from scratch to arrange how money should be supplied to a democratic society – nobody in their right mind would dream of setting it up as it is now. Anyone with an inkling of how to manage anything would know that merging the two conflicting functions of

- providing the public money supply competently and fairly on behalf of society as a whole, and
- encouraging commercial banks to compete for profit in the market for lending and borrowing money,

would destroy the efficiency and reliability of both functions.

The root question is: what is the best way to create and manage the national money supply in a democracy? It is not primarily a technical banking question, as politicians and experts still assume as they struggle to decide what should now be done.[1]

Nobody denies that reforming how the national money supply is provided and managed will, in today's circumstances, have serious consequences for the banks. Those must be recognised. But, as with most practical problems, it will be sensible to put the horse before the cart.

Key questions about the national money supply
Root question
What is the best way to create and manage the national money supply in a democracy?
Important factual questions
Who creates the money supply and puts it into circulation?
In what form do they create it: as debt, or free of debt?
Who gets first use of it?
For what purposes?
Important practical questions
Who should create it and put it into circulation?
In what form should they create it: as debt, or free of debt?
Who should get first use of it?
For what purposes?

1. An example of present conventional thinking has been that the terms of reference of the recent UK Independent Commission on Banking didn't include 'Who should create the national money supply, and in what form?'. No wonder that its final recommendations have been seen as inadequate by people with the common interest at heart, and seen at the same time as damagingly costly and cumbersome by the banking industry itself. See http://tinyurl.com/3acopaa, http://tinyurl.com/88u5zqd and http://tinyurl.com/7djyx4w.

The present arrangement

In the UK – and the situation is similar in other countries – we allow our governments to make us dependent on commercial banks to create 97% of our national money supply as debt. Our governments don't have to do that; no law says they must; and, even if a law did say it, we could change it.

Most people don't yet recognise that the banks create the money by writing it out of nothing into our bank accounts as interest-bearing loans. The experts call it 'creating credit', obscuring the fact that actually – as shown in the official statistics – the banks are being unnecessarily allowed to create almost all the national money supply as bank-account money for their own profit.

They do it under what is known as 'fractional reserve banking'. It requires commercial banks to keep in reserve only a fraction of the money that has been deposited with them. For example, if the required fraction is 10%, a deposit into the banking system of £1000 would allow it to create an addition of £900 to the money supply by lending it to customers as 'credit', and then a further 10% of £900, and then a further . . . and so on.

Meanwhile the Bank of England and Royal Mint, as national agencies still providing national money as a public service in the public interest, are reduced to creating only about 3% of it as banknotes and coins. These bring in a correspondingly small contribution to public revenue.[2]

In striking contrast to the £multi-billion annual subsidy that our government gives to the bankers by allowing them to create almost all the money supply out of nothing as loans into customers' bank accounts, it severely punishes anyone other than the Bank of England or Royal Mint who creates and issues banknotes and coins. Anyone who fakes banknotes and coins and puts them into circulation as genuine money commits a crime – forgery or counterfeiting. If found guilty they go to prison while dozens of millionaire commercial bankers stay free, enjoying the profitable privileges that come from creating all the rest of the money supply.[3]

---

2. In pre-democratic societies it was kings and rulers who provided all the currency. Their income from doing so was called seignorage (see Chapter 1), and they spent it as they decided. No expert economic knowledge is needed to see that corresponding arrangements in today's democracies would treat all the income from creating new money as public revenue, and that normal democratic budgetary procedures would decide on its first use. 3. For more on the penalties for counterfeiting and forgery, see Darius Guppy at http://tinyurl.com/y9glcec.

A lesson from the history of banknotes

For 160 years or so, our leaders have suppressed and ignored the important lesson to be learned from the history of banknotes.

This lesson has been mentioned in the book already. But it so important for us to understand it in the context of this chapter that it needs to be emphasised. Banknotes originated as credit notes issued by individual banks to their customers as receipts, promising to repay the gold and silver coins and bullion deposited with them by their customers for safe-keeping. Over the centuries, bank customers found that exchanging these paper notes was an easier way to make payments to one another than physically transferring the bulky metal money held for them by their banks. In the course of time, banks developed their credit notes to meet that demand, and eventually exchanging credit notes as a means of payment spread so widely that for practical purposes they became money.

Meanwhile, the banks had been learning that, when all went well, comparatively few of their customers would redeem their credit notes; most would leave their gold and silver money untouched in the bank. So the banks found they could profit by issuing credit notes worth more than the value of the gold and silver money they held for their customers. And that is what they did.

From time to time this resulted in 'a run on the bank'. The customers of a bank would realise that it had issued more paper money than it would be able to repay from the gold and silver money it was holding in its vaults. Fearing that they might lose their precious-metal money that was in the bank, their customers would rush to it to take their money out before other customers took out theirs. Their 'run' would bring about the disaster they all feared. The bank would go bust.

By the middle of the 19th century it had become clear in England that what had originated as the credit notes of private banks were now almost universally used as actual money, and that failure to control their issue was damaging the economy as a whole. So the Bank Charter Act of 1844 was passed, leading to the present Bank of England monopoly of the banknote issue in England and Wales and requiring commercial banks in Scotland and Northern Ireland to back the value of the banknotes they still issue themselves by holdings of Bank of England notes.

British banknotes still say "I promise to pay. . .", but we know that that is just a historic survival, and they are no longer simple credit notes. A joker trying to redeem them from the Bank of England will be sent away with a flea in the ear or, at best, with other banknotes to the same value as those presented for redemption – or even the same ones – minus commission maybe!

So what lesson from the history of banknotes have the managers of the public money system ignored? It is fairly simple.

Since 1844 commercial banks have been allowed to develop exactly the same trick with bank-account credit as they had previously done with credit notes. Credit notes had developed into paper money conveying value created out of nothing. They had circulated *outside the banking system* in person-to-person transactions between bank customers, as banknotes still do. When the issue of banknotes was transferred to the Bank of England – later nationalised as an agency of the state in 1946 – other commercial banks were deprived of that source of profit.

So, having been deprived of that source of profit in 1844, how have the banks nonetheless achieved the astonishing further growth in the proportion of the national money supply that they now create as interest-bearing, profit-making loans?

They have done it by writing it as credit lent into their customers' bank accounts inside the banking system instead of, as previously, into banknotes circulating in the outside world. They have enabled their customers to spend it into circulation by paying it directly from their bank accounts into the bank accounts of other bank customers, and it continues to circulate that way *within the banking system* until the loan is repaid. Then it is written off, the money goes back into the nothing from which it originated, and new bank loans replace it in the money supply.

That development has helped the bankers and their associates to obscure how our money is created and put into circulation; and the dematerialisation of bank-account money into electronic form has mystified it further in the past half-century.

So today, everyone with a current bank account knows that we can spend the money in it immediately, just like the coins in our pockets and the banknotes in our wallets. But few of us realise that the money in our bank accounts originated as profit-making loans from banks and that, as we hold it and circulate it through the economy, we are paying them interest on it.

Interconnected effects of the present arrangement

(1) We now pay a hidden subsidy to the banks[4]

This follows directly from the last paragraph. As debt-created money circulates through the economy, it pays interest to the banks that created it. It is the original borrowers who actually pay it. But the prices charged by borrowers who have borrowed it to finance the production and provision of goods and services for sale must include in their prices the cost of paying interest on it and eventually repaying it. So almost everyone who buys anything will indirectly be paying a fee to the banks for using money the banks had created as debt.

This is a kind of 'stealth tax'. But it's not a tax we pay to the government as public revenue. Under the present way of providing the money supply, everyone pays it as a subsidy to the banks almost every time we use money in the course of our daily lives. That includes the government's use of money on behalf of society as a whole.

Conveniently for the banks and those who share significantly in bank profits, the statistics don't show how much this present annual subsidy is worth to the banks. Nor do they show how much public revenue will be gained – for the benefit of taxpayers and other citizens – when an agency of the state takes over the function of creating the money supply debt-free and giving it to the government to spend on public purposes. Creating the money supply free of debt will relieve everyone of the need to pay that money to the banks.

It will still be true, of course, that business borrowers will have to pay bank interest on loans needed to cover the production costs of the goods and services they sell to us, and their prices to us will have to include those loan costs. But for two reasons the total amounts we now pay the banks for using money will fall.

(a) First, those loan costs will tend to fall, because the rates of interest the banks can charge will be based on a more competitive money market than today's, which protects the existing banks from competition. This is discussed later in this chapter under the heading 'Lending, borrowing and saving after monetary reform'.
(b) Second, the money supply will no longer be forced to grow, as it is now.

---

4. This is only one of the many ways governments now make taxpayers subsidise the banks. Some others are discussed by the new economics foundation at http://tinyurl.com/7dvyl9q.

(2) Why the money supply is now forced to grow

When customers now repay loans to their banks, the banks write off the money and return it to the nothing from which they had originally created it. But the money that has been paid on it as interest remains in existence as the property of the banks.

This makes it continually necessary for enough new money to be lent into existence to replace *both* what was originally lent but has now been written off *plus* what has gone to the banks as interest on it. Otherwise there will not be enough money in circulation to support the non-financial activities of the economy.

The present arrangement for providing the money supply thus requires the money supply to grow continually. That is one reason why governments in normal times instruct the Bank of England to maintain a continuing inflation rate[5] of between 1% and 3% a year, rather than money values that stay stable.

Whether economic growth can any longer be accepted as an overriding purpose of the money system in the 21st century has been questioned in Chapter 2, concluding that it should not be, partly because:

(a) the volume of economic activity, dependent on the total value of money circulating through the economy, cannot grow *ad infinitum*, and
(b) it involves a continually growing volume of money transactions that banks and other financial businesses profit from at the expense of everyone else.

(3) Indebtedness in society is forced to grow

As the present arrangement for creating the money supply necessitates its continual increase and depends on people and businesses taking out loans from the banks, it automatically causes rising indebtedness in society. Bank of England statistics confirm that the growth of the 'Broad Money Supply' and the 'Debt Owed by the Public in the UK' totalled roughly £2,500bn between 1969 and 2009, and closely matched each other's growth year by year.[6] This inevitably has a further undesirable consequence.

---

5. The rate at which money loses its value for what it can buy. 6. Source: Bank of England Interactive Statistical Database figures for 'M4 and M4 Lending'. See page 19 of Submission to the Independent Commission on Banking, November 2010: http://tinyurl.com/3vqfvws.

(4) National poverty must increase

You don't have to be the proverbial rocket scientist – or even a professional economist or statistician – to figure out who, apart from the banks themselves, will benefit most from increasing indebtedness in society and who will suffer most.

In general, those who benefit most will be people and businesses with enough spare money to lend or invest it and get back more money from doing so. Those who suffer most will be those who have to borrow money at interest, and so pay more in order to meet the needs of themselves and their families. In short, the present way of providing the money supply systematically works to increase poverty and widen the gap between rich and poor.

(5) Ecologically damaging human activity must grow

Because the present way of providing the money supply necessitates continual growth of debt and of conventionally measured economic production, it has the general effect of making us earn our living by extracting and wasting more of the Earth's resources than would otherwise be needed. Although it may be argued theoretically that the need for continually increasing economic growth and debt repayment could be met by a shift to 'green' and 'weightless' financial growth, we know that in practice things don't work out like that.

That is partly because providing a money supply based on debt widens the gap between rich and poor (4 above). But it is also because it encourages increasing numbers of very rich people to behave like masters of the universe, enjoying ecologically damaging lifestyles with yachts, expensive houses and other lavish back-up all over the world, supported by the luxury of tax havens; and because at the same time it compels millions of the world's poor to work in unecological and often slavish occupations as the only available way of gaining a living for themselves and their families.

(6) Banking efficiency will continue to suffer

Banking efficiency is central to the flow of money through the economy. Subsidising banks as highly as we now do allows banks to coexist comfortably with their existing competitors and to discourage potentially more innovative and competitive new entrants from coming into the banking industry.

Whereas providing the national money supply is a service that needs to be managed efficiently in the public interest with a sense of public service, the market for borrowing and lending money needs to operate freely and efficiently in the interests of its customers. The present way of managing both the supply of money and the market for money already in circulation fails on both counts, and the efficiency of the economy suffers from both as a result.

(7) Economic distortions

Allowing banks to decide, in their own commercial interest, how the national money they create will be used on its first entry into circulation has damaging consequences. We need not blame the banks for it. If they are given the chance, it is natural for them to distort the initial flows of money through the economy in favour of activities likely to be profitable to them. Here are some examples.

(a) It encourages lending for speculative purposes.
Banks often find it more profitable to create money to lend to people and businesses to buy already existing assets – like land and houses, and stocks and shares – for speculative purposes, than to finance the production of goods and provision of services to support productive work in progress or new developments of benefit to the economy and society.

However, house-price booms and busts are only partly due to how the money supply is now managed. Another cause is the failure to tax land values and so recapture – as public revenue – the public money spent on local infrastructure and facilities. Without a tax on land values, that public money automatically finds its way into windfall profits to local property owners.

So monetary reform would not by itself solve that particular problem. Although banks would then have to borrow all the money they lend, they might still find it more attractive to borrow it to lend to speculative buyers of already existing properties than to borrow it to lend for more beneficial purposes. This and other combinations of faulty monetary and tax policies are further discussed in Chapter 4.

(b) It discourages the development of local currencies in support of more self-reliant local economies (see Chapter 6).

Allowing commercial banks to create virtually all the national currency as profit-making debt obliges the borrowers to earn national currency in order to service and eventually repay the debt. Perpetuating the need for borrowers to earn and pay national currency for that purpose is bound to discourage the spread of parallel community currencies and other aspects of local financial self-reliance.

On the other hand, when the money supply has all been converted into a circulating fund of debt-free money created by the central bank and given to the government to spend into circulation debt-free, it will be easier for governments to spend more of it as limited initial grants to encourage a growing number of local people to develop the use of local currencies; and those will be able to support other local financial enterprises like local development banks in support of more economically self-reliant localities.[7] In general it is easier for governments than commercial banks to spend money debt-free on public purposes; after all, that is how most government spending is spent.

(c) There is an important broader point at issue here.

Projects of high long-term value to society as a whole, but of no short-term profit to banks or other commercial businesses, will naturally not be selected as first users of money created as loans by commercial banks. Money is much more likely to be targeted on projects of that kind if the money has been created by a public agency and spent into circulation debt-free by a democratic government in the public interest.

Health care is a good example: sophisticated new drugs from pharmaceutical corporations designed for treating sicknesses when they have happened or preventing them happening are more likely to attract banks to create loan money to invest in them, than are new programmes of health creation to prevent sickness occurring. More generally, responding to bad things after they have occurred, or when conditions that encourage them are already threatening, will usually be more profitable and attract higher investment of money than measures to remove the ultimate causes of those bad things and prevent them happening at all. *Crime* and *war* are other examples.

7. UK Prime Minister David Cameron's idea of the 'Big Society' cannot be effective until the privilege is withdrawn that now means Big Money dominates our lives.

The interconnected effects of the present arrangement	
Hidden subsidy paid to banks	Almost everyone who buys anything will indirectly be paying a fee to the banks for using money the banks had created as debt. This can be seen as a type of stealth tax.
Money supply forced to grow	In order to support the non-financial activities of the economy, enough new money has to be lent into existence to replace both what was originally lent but has now been written off plus what has gone to the banks as interest on it.
Indebtedness forced to grow	The increase in money supply depends on people and businesses taking out loans from the banks which automatically causes rising indebtedness in society.
Growth of poverty	Increased indebtedness benefits those with money to lend or invest and hurts those who have to borrow to meet their needs.
Increase in ecological damage	The continual growth of debt and of conventionally measured economic production involves the extraction and waste of more of the Earth's resources.
Strain on economic efficiency	The subsidising of banks reduces the efficiency of the banking system and consequently of the whole national economy.
Economic distortions	Allowing the banks to decide how the money they create will be used on its first entry into circulation creates problems like excessive lending for speculative purposes and an ignoring of projects that have a high long-term value to society.

A regular cause of financial instability

Crises of financial instability are the inevitable result of mixing together the two conflicting functions of

- providing the public money supply in the interest of society as a whole, and
- competing for profit in the commercial market for lending and borrowing money.

Bernard Lietaer and his colleagues have recorded that, worldwide, there have been almost 100 major financial crises over the past twenty years.[8] We are now, it seems, stumbling into the consequences of what may turn out to be the most damaging financial breakdown humanity has ever seen. As

8. http://tinyurl.com/7t2x8bj.

Lietaer reminds us, the last one on anything like this scale was followed by the Great Depression of the 1930s, an international wave of fascism, and the Second World War.

This present worldwide financial boom and bust has developed in three stages – boom, bust, and aftermath. At the time of writing, the second and third are both with us.

There is either ignorance or deliberate concealment by the managers of the money system about the flows of money in those three stages: where did the money come from, where has it gone to, and where is it still continuing to go to? In all three stages huge windfalls – at the cost of the rest of society – appear to have been enjoyed by a limited number of bankers, other financial managers, their associates in connected walks of life like accountancy and financial law, and their families and friends. We should press our elected representatives, executive government and professionals in charge of the money system to admit that that correctly reflects what has been happening.

Stage 1. Boom-time. In a time of boom it is in the public interest to limit the supply of money going into the economy. But it's obvious that, if naturally profit-seeking commercial bankers are entrusted with creating the national money supply as profit-making loans, they won't be able to resist competing with one another to create and lend as much as they can for as long as the boom goes on. By doing that they can make themselves very rich – Windfall Number 1. They are bound to stoke up the boom – and so speed up the onset of the bust that will end it.

In 2007 the Chief Executive Officer of Citibank graphically described the bankers' situation. Shortly before he got his multi-million-dollar 'golden parachute' to compensate him for being 'chucked out' of his crisis-stricken bank, Chuck Prince explained: "As long as the music is playing, you've got to get up and dance." I recalled having seen bankers stampeding toward the abyss into which many of them knew they would probably fall, when I was director of the Inter-Bank Research Organisation during the much smaller secondary banking crisis of the early 1970s. I understood very well what Chuck Prince meant.

Stage 2. Bust-time. When booms go bust, as they always do, the public need becomes the opposite of what it was in the boom. We need more money put into circulation, not less. At this point our self-inflicted dependence on commercial banks to provide the money supply again works in the wrong direction – the opposite direction to the one that was wrong in the boom.

Banks now can't or won't provide enough money.

They have lost so much that many are in danger of going bust and out of business altogether. Because our governments unnecessarily require us to depend on the banks to provide the national money supply, the bankers are now able to hold us to ransom. Our governments have to bail out the banks with billions of our public money – trillions worldwide – Windfall Number 2.

However, at this stage the bailed-out banks can't or won't concentrate on the task of creating and lending the amount of money the economy needs in order to revive. They must use most of the bail-out money for themselves.

First, they must use it to strengthen their balance sheets, to protect them from going bust in the future; to do that they have to set aside money as reserves with the central bank. Second, they need to spend much of the rest of the bail-out money on competing with one another to give big enough bonuses to their managers to persuade them not to go to other more generous banks. In November 2009, for example, a few months after paying back the US bail-out money it had received,[9] the Chairman and CEO of Goldman Sachs was preparing to hand out more than $20 billion in year-end bonuses to his managers – claiming that his bank had only been doing "God's work"!

Now, in 2012, nobody in the whole wide world with responsibility for managing national money supplies has seemed able to suggest a practical way to solve the puzzle. So, if the banks cannot or will not create enough money by lending it, what might be a better way to create it and put it into circulation?

Some, like Niall Ferguson and Laurence Kotlikoff in 'How to take the moral hazard out of banking', opting for *limited purpose banking* as the answer, are coming near to the only sensible solution of the puzzle.[10] More importantly, Bank of England Governor Sir Mervyn King appears to be almost prepared to accept that a different way of creating and managing the money supply is what is needed. On 25 October 2010 in a public lecture in New York,[11] he drew attention to the possibility of "eliminating fractional reserve banking".[12] He recognised that "the pretence that risk-free deposits can be supported by risky assets is alchemy". He concluded that "of all the many ways

---

9. From TARP, the $700 billion Troubled Asset Relief Program launched under President Bush's Emergency Economic Stabilization Act of 2008. 10. http://tinyurl.com/87jsxvv.

11. See http://tinyurl.com/3xg69gj. 12. As noted earlier, fractional reserve banking is what we have now. It requires commercial banks to keep in reserve only a fraction of the money deposited with them. For example, if the required fraction is 10%, a deposit into the banking system of £1,000 would allow it to create an addition of £900 to the money supply by lending it to customers as 'credit', and then a further 10% of £900, and then a further . . . and so on.

of organising banking, the worst is the one we have today."

However, at successive international meetings of the Group of Twenty countries (G20) and similar gatherings, the mountains – to paraphrase the poet Horace[13] – have been labouring with great energy and cost without bringing even a ridiculous mouse to birth. In fact, what has come to birth is the third and most potentially damaging stage of the continuing crisis.

Stage 3. 'Sovereign Debt'. This third stage in the present financial breakdown that began in 2007/08 is now overlapping the second and is still developing. It is particularly affecting the eurozone, but that is threatening the wider global money system too. This is how it works.

When governments have to borrow the money to bail out the banks, the national debt (or sovereign debt) grows.[14] Then governments have to raise enough money from their taxpayers and other citizens (by increasing taxes and cutting public spending) to service the debt until it has been paid back and reduced to an acceptable level. When countries themselves – not just their banks – reach a level of debt higher than potential lenders trust them to service and pay back, they have to be bailed out.

That has already happened to the governments of Greece, Ireland and Portugal; and it is threatening other eurozone countries and the future of the eurozone itself. It has also resulted in the need for Emergency Budgets elsewhere, including the UK, causing widespread hardship and serious social unrest.

Taking the UK as an example, the UK Total Government Debt in 2001 was £300bn; in 2009 it had doubled to £600bn and early in 2012 it had risen to over £1 trillion. At present the annual interest the government is paying on the debt is £43bn. It was expected to rise to at least £70bn by 2015, before the UK Emergency Budget was introduced in June 2010; and the impact of that Budget on the eventual figure is as uncertain as is its impact on everything else by 2015.[15]

The growth of government debt has been part of a wider growth of indebtedness across the whole economy. In 1987 the UK's total debt for households, the City, non-financial companies and the government stood at 200% of gross domestic product; by 2009 it had reached £7.5 trillion, 540% of GDP.[16]

---

13. "Parturient montes, nascetur ridiculus mus." Horace, *Ars Poetica* (183). 14. 'Government debt', 'national debt', 'sovereign debt', and 'public debt' all mean much the same thing. It should not be confused with the 'total debt' of a country, which includes the debt of financial institutions, non-financial businesses and households in addition to government debt. 15. http://tinyurl.com/3x3kk7f. 16. http://tinyurl.com/26u4k3k.

This massive growth of indebtedness has been hugely profitable for bankers already. As interest continues to be paid on the debts, and more of the outstanding capital gets paid off, more profit will continue to flow in their direction – Windfall Number 3.

Even if some experts may qualify or dispute some technical details of that brief summary, two things appear to be certain.

(1) If the conventional thinking of governments and their expert advisers had recognised how much public spending could be saved and how much public revenue could be raised by a simple, radical monetary reform on the following lines, measures like the UK Emergency Budget of June 2010 could have meant much less unnecessary hardship for most UK citizens than they are now causing.

(2) The necessary monetary reform, as described in the section immediately following, has become all the more urgent now as an emergency measure to control the unpredictable worldwide damage threatened by the crisis that continues to develop. The first step to it could be the immediate introduction of the next tranche in the 'quantitative easing' programmes of central banks;[17] the Bank of England is expected to complete £275bn of quantitative easing early in 2012. But this time the new money should be put directly into circulation in the real economy, for example via a Citizen's Income (Chapter 4), instead of via further bail-outs to banks and the financial sector. It could be done very quickly indeed, almost immediately, once the decision had been made.

Monetary reform: separating the two functions

A simple basic reform is all that is needed to separate the two functions now confused. It has two complementary parts.

(1) It will transfer to nationalised central banks like the Bank of England the responsibility for creating, not just banknotes and coins as now, but also the overwhelmingly large component of the supply of public money consisting of bank-account money mainly held and transmitted electronically. Having created the money, the central bank will give it to the

17. Like the Bank of England in the UK, the Fed in the USA, and the European Central Bank in the eurozone.

government to spend it into circulation on public purposes under standard democratic budgetary procedures.

(2) It will prohibit anyone else, including commercial banks, from creating bank-account money out of thin air, just as forging metal coins and counterfeiting paper banknotes are criminal offences.

Those two measures together will nationalise the national money supply and make it possible to denationalise any commercial banks that have had to be nationalised. They will then be able to compete freely with all the other commercial banks in a much more open profit-based market for borrowing and lending money that is already in circulation after its creation by the central bank.

The first of those two measures will make a public agency responsible for directly creating and managing the public money supply in the public interest.

The second will create a much more competitive market than now for facilitating loans between lenders and borrowers. The loss of the commercial banks' privilege of creating the money they lend will bring them into line with ordinary private-sector businesses that don't get given their main materials as a free gift. It will encourage them to provide better services more efficiently than now to their customers, and make it easier for new entrants to join the payment services industry. Anyone who genuinely accepts the virtues of a free-market economy, subject to rules fairly laid down and enforced by democratic governments in the public interest, should support it.

Most taxpayers and other citizens will benefit from:

(1) getting rid of the hidden tax that we all now pay to commercial banks every day as interest on all the bank-account money in circulation; and

(2) profiting from the one-off increase in public revenue resulting from the process of converting the money supply created by commercial banks as debt into money created free of debt by the Bank of England as an addition to public revenue for use according to normal democratic budgetary procedures, either to reduce otherwise necessary taxes or to be spent into circulation on public purposes.

The published national and bank statistics do not provide financial estimates for what those two benefits would amount to.[18] But conservative assumptions of 5% annual interest payments and an existing total money

18. The Treasury and Bank of England should be asked to publish their best estimates.

supply of £1,500 billion to be replaced would provide:

(1) an annual total saving to all citizens of, say, £75 billion, and
(2) a one-off benefit to the public purse totalling some £1,500 billion over a 3-year period of transition from the existing commercial-bank-created money supply to the new debt-free money supply created to serve the public interest.[19]

The hardships imposed by the continuing financial crisis on the majority of citizens who were not directly responsible for it, and the continuing public unrest resulting from them, bring an added sense of emergency to the overwhelming long-term arguments for monetary reform.

Controlling the money supply after monetary reform

Transferring responsibility for creating all new bank-account money to the central bank will catch up with what happened to banknotes under the Bank Charter Act of 1844 in the UK.[20] It will be the natural next step in the historical evolution of the Bank of England, following the operational independence given to it in 1997. The private bank established in 1694 to serve the needs of the monarch will step-by-step have turned into a national agency responsible for providing a money supply that serves the common interests of all the citizens of a democratic society.

After the reform, operationally independent central banks like the Bank of England will continue to be given published monetary policy objectives by their governments. But they will no longer be expected to achieve them indirectly by managing interest rates to influence the demand for new money created by banks as loans under the system of fractional reserve banking.[21] They will themselves decide at regular intervals how much new money needs to be added to the money supply, and then create it and pass it as debt-free public revenue to the government.

Then the government will either use it to reduce taxation or put it into circulation by spending it on public purposes along with other public revenue, in accordance with normal budgeting procedures. Normally the central bank will play no part in deciding how the money which it creates to meet monetary policy objectives will be spent.

---

19. The estimate of £200 billion at www.bendyson.com/statistics therefore seems very moderate.
20. See p. 100. 21. See p. 99.

The money supply will change its character when it all consists of debt-free money created by the central bank. As the new debt-free money comes into circulation, and as the repayment of existing bank loans extinguishes the money created by the commercial banks, it will become a clearly defined fund of officially created and recognised money.

This will consist of three categories of money:

(1) banknotes and coins;
(2) sight deposits in the current accounts of customers of banks and other agencies licensed by the central bank to manage bank accounts for customers; and
(3) the money in the current accounts of those banks and agencies with the central bank.

Those will constitute a supply of actual money in circulation which is immediately available for spending, and the total of which will be precisely identifiable in the official statistics.

One particular point about this new arrangement should be noted. If ever the central bank decided that the money supply should be reduced by withdrawing money from it, it could ask the government to pay back the required reduction out of public revenue from taxes and other sources. The central bank would then destroy it.

As long as the need for continual growth of the money supply as an aspect of continual economic growth has been taken for granted, the question of how to reduce the money supply has been irrelevant. But it will become more relevant, if unending economic growth comes to be recognised as undesirable and indeed impossible, as discussed in Chapter 2.

Lending, borrowing and saving after monetary reform

The fund of money constituting the money supply will become quite distinct from financial claims, such as savings in savings accounts. Those will not contain money. They will be claims for money to be paid to their holders at certain times in certain circumstances. They will have been bought by their holders paying money for them to their sellers, as other forms of saving like investments, securities, insurance policies etc. are bought now. Some claims like insurance policies pay back sums of money on specified dates or events;

others, like share certificates, are exchangeable for money at their market prices at pay-back time.

In the transition after monetary reform, as borrowers repay bank loans borrowed before the reform came into force, money to replace that money in the money supply will have been created by the central bank, and given to the government to spend into circulation. When it then reaches some people and organisations they may decide to save it, not spend it. Their banks may then borrow it from them and lend it to borrowers, no longer creating new money in the process but as plain intermediaries borrowing existing money from lenders and then lending it at a profit to borrowers – as most people mistakenly suppose they do now.

Customers saving money with a bank will pay it to the bank as the purchase price of a claim to receive money later at a specified date with a specified rate of interest paid at specified intervals. The principle will be that money in the circulating fund of national money cannot be simultaneously available for spending to more than one holder at a time. The fund of money in circulation will remain unchanged in size, except for increases or withdrawals made by the central bank in accordance with the government's monetary policy objectives.

The commercial banks, having hitherto been able to create money as soon as their customers ask to borrow it, will face the need for efficient stock control – just as all other businesses need to make their ranges of products and services available to meet customer demand as quickly as possible, without the cost of having too much on hand for too long. The only difference is that for banks, being single-product (money) businesses, this will be a much simpler challenge than for others like supermarkets.

Moreover, the need to find existing money quickly to lend to retail banks so that they can lend it quickly to their customers will encourage money markets to develop ways to find it quickly. Even if it does lead to some loss of flexibility for banks and their customers, and slightly slow down the velocity of money circulation, the central bank will be able to compensate for that by increasing the money supply. So there is no reason why it should damage the public interest if that happens.

The regulatory consequences

The monetary reform proposed in this chapter reflects "the attraction of the more radical solutions . . . that they offer the hope of avoiding the seemingly inevitable drift to ever more complex and costly regulation" – Governor of the Bank of England Sir Mervyn King's words in his New York lecture of 25 October 2010.[22] For its contrast with the expected regulatory aftermath of less radical solutions, see the jungle of proposals being discussed by the Bank and other UK financial organisations in May 2011.[23]

Monetary reform will make it possible to clarify responsibilities for regulation, supervision and guarantees on the following lines. They will be based on the differences between three separate sets of functions:

- the central bank's responsibility for providing and managing the national supply of money as a distinct, well defined circulating fund, the value of which will be guaranteed by the state,
- the responsibilities of government agencies and departments for raising public revenue and spending it on public purposes, as at present, and
- private-sector, profit-making activities of buying and selling the very wide range of claims to money which, while being bought and sold for money, will not – after monetary reform – themselves contain money immediately available for spending by their purchasers.

The first of these three areas of regulation and supervision will be the responsibility of the central bank. It will include:

- licensing banks (and other organisations) to provide payments services in the national currency,
- regulating and supervising the administration and activities of those organisations,
- ensuring by audit trails that they do not create new money, and
- guaranteeing all deposits in their current accounts.

The central bank will continue to be accountable to the elected government and parliament for how it carries out these functions.

The second area – public revenue raising and public spending – will remain,

22. http://tinyurl.com/3xg69gj. 23. http://tinyurl.com/7uxloec.

as now, a responsibility of executive government departments democratically controlled by elected ministers and accountable to parliament. It will include guaranteeing the value of financial claims sold by agencies of the government like National Savings.

In the third area of regulation and supervision – of private-sector financial services – monetary reform will abolish the "seemingly inevitable drift to ever more complex and costly regulation" of commercial banks creating money under the fractional reserve system; the banks will be prohibited from creating money altogether.[24]

That means that after monetary reform this third area of regulation will be concerned with how financial private-sector businesses handle money, in much the same way as non-financial businesses are regulated that handle money when buying and selling other things. They will simply be receiving money or paying money in exchange for the other things they sell or buy.

Private-sector financial businesses will no longer be creating new money and putting it into circulation, thereby affecting the stability of the money supply. Therefore, no guarantees from public funds need be given for the contractual or estimated values of the financial claims they buy and sell, any more than guarantees from public funds need be given for the reliability of other goods and services bought or sold by other types of business. Buyers and sellers should buy and sell them at their own risk, subject to the criminal and civil law, and laws on consumer protection. There will no longer be a need for special, complicated financial regulations to control their activities, as if they were still playing a core role in creating the money supply.

Because it will be new, the point here may be worth repeating. The financial claims that commercial banks and other financial enterprises will be selling after monetary reform will contain no real money themselves that is available for immediate use. They will just be selling claims to be paid money in the future. They will include the savings and lending services provided by banks to their customers, and all kinds of insurance policies, stock exchanges, commodity markets, pension funds and many others dealing in financial

---

24. See foonote 8 on page 32 for the parallel between the radical reform of the world's money system needed now and the 16th-century Copernican revolution in our understanding of the solar system. The complex regulations needed at present by the unreformed money system match the epicycles piled on epicycles needed then to correct the consequences of pre-Copernican, Ptolemaic astronomy.

claims. They will tend to shade into activities that have been called 'casino banking' – hedge funds, trading in derivatives, options, futures, etc.

After monetary reform there should be no need to make a clear distinction between those financial claims and others arising from forms of gambling controlled by the Gambling Commission, or betting on horse-racing and other sports. Trading on the stock-market, or in gold, or on the fine art and antiques market, and countless other trading activities too, involve a measure of gambling and can continue to be governed by regulations of their own. Subject to those regulations and to the criminal and civil law and laws on consumer protection, buyers and sellers should be expected to buy and sell them at their own risk.

Responsibilities for regulation, supervision and guarantees

1. Providing and managing the national supply of money

The central bank will continue to be accountable to the elected government and parliament for:

- licensing banks and others to provide payments services
- regulating and supervising their administration and activities
- ensuring by audit trails that they do not create new money
- guaranteeing all deposits in their current accounts.

2. Public revenue raising and public spending

This will remain, as now, a responsibility of executive government democratically controlled by elected ministers and accountable to parliament.

3. Responsibility for regulating private sector financial services

As banks and other enterprises will be prohibited from creating money altogether, the need for special financial regulation and supervision will be significantly reduced, if not altogether abolished. The buying and selling of financial claims will be treated like the buying and selling of all other products and services.

International competition and the national economy

Commercial banks and their supporters in the UK and other countries claim that withdrawing the present subsidy they get from creating the national money supply would put them at a disadvantage against competitors from other countries; for example, that it "would lead to the migration from the

City of London of the largest collection of banks in the world, and be a disaster for the British economy".[25] They say that UK banks and the wider financial services industry create exceptionally large shares of wealth (GDP), tax revenue, and employment for our economy, without which we would all suffer.[26]

But it is high time for active citizens to insist that the government must examine those claims thoroughly. We must press MPs and ministers to publish the answers to the following questions:

- how much does having such a dominant and highly subsidised financial sector benefit most UK citizens compared with what it costs us – economically, socially and ecologically? [27]
- how many UK citizens positively benefit from it, and how many of us suffer?
- which citizens benefit from it, and which suffer?
- how realistic is it to claim that top bankers and other financial people and businesses will decide to leave the country and go elsewhere if monetary reform is introduced in Britain before other countries catch up?
- how welcome would they be elsewhere if they left the UK?
- how much would it matter to our own economy and society if they left the UK? and
- should we press ahead with reforming the way our money supply is created and managed, without waiting until countries lagging behind us agree to reform theirs too?

My answer is that we citizens of the UK, and of most other countries too, should insist that our governments reform the way our national money supply is created as soon as possible. We should none of us wait for other countries to catch up with us. [28]

---

25. The view of Michael Portillo when Shadow Chancellor: see *Monetary reform – making it happen*, p. 41, www.jamesrobertson.com/books.htm#monetary. 26. 'Economic Contribution of UK Financial Services 2010', www.thecityuk.com. 27. Research by the new economics foundation in 2009 found that "while collecting salaries of between £500,000 and £10 million, leading City bankers destroy £7 of social value for every pound in value they generate." See 'A Bit Rich: Calculating the real value to society of different professions', www.neweconomics.org/publications/bit-rich. 28. What we should do about international monetary reform is discussed in Chapter 5.

Key questions for the government to answer
What are the costs vs benefits for UK citizens – economically, socially and ecologically – of having such a dominant and highly subsidised financial sector?
How many UK citizens positively benefit from it, and how many of us suffer?
How realistic is it to claim that top bankers and other financial people and businesses will go elsewhere if monetary reform is introduced in Britain before other countries catch up?
Would they be welcome elsewhere if they left the UK?
How much would it matter to our own economy and society if they left the UK?
Should we wait to reform the way our money supply is created and managed until other economically important countries agree to reform theirs simultaneously? Or have we left it too late, already?

The eurozone crisis

The eurozone crisis is the latest phase in the third stage (Sovereign-Debt-Out-Of-Control) that has followed the banking collapse of 2007/08. At the time of writing, the possibility is growing that Greece may be the first country to leave the eurozone. If it does so and brings back the drachma as its national currency, the Greek government should seriously consider adopting a reformed monetary regime on the lines proposed in this chapter.

The Greeks are a proud people. By making good use of the otherwise insoluble eurozone crisis, they could pioneer the new path into the future – for themselves, for other European countries and eventually for the rest of the world.

Conclusion

This chapter began by asking the right questions. Having now reached the chapter's end, we find that answering them gives us the answer to other questions that have attracted public and expert concern in recent months. One of these is what to do about bankers' bonuses; another is whether to break up the banks so that they will no longer be 'too big to fail'.

The answers are: the bankers' bonuses scandal shows top bankers today to be badly out of touch with the values and demands of modern democratic societies; and today's banking system, dominated by a small number of world-scale banks, highly subsidised and protected by the privilege of creating money out of nothing as profit-making debt, should give way to a worldwide system of smaller banks competing with one another to serve the needs of their customers.

The effective practical course for people who share that view is to recognise the root of the problem. Reforming how the money supply is now created and managed will remove our self-inflicted dependence on big banks that means that we cannot let them fail. It will generate competitive pressures on them to decentralise. It will remove the huge subsidies – far greater than any other industry we can think of – which now protect them from those pressures, and which they now channel into absurdly high salaries and bonuses for themselves.

In short, we have to accept that there is no way to make the present misconceived arrangement for creating the money supply work satisfactorily. Monetary reform, as proposed in this chapter, will avoid further costly and fruitless, national and international consultations on how to square that circle. It will liberate us to develop a more democratic, decentralised money system serving the majority of citizens, not just a favoured minority that benefits from the subsidised profits of the financial sector.

Meanwhile, the worsening global monetary crisis that continues to develop from the banking collapse of 2007/08 now calls for emergency action. The clearly necessary immediate response, as mentioned earlier in this chapter, is for the 'quantitative easing' programmes of central banks[29] to create new money to be put into circulation directly into the real economy – for example via a Citizen's Income – and not in further bail-outs to banks and the financial sector. Once the decision is made that it is the only responsible course of action and must be done urgently, it can be done almost immediately.

A simple thought should end this chapter. The obvious way to reduce our public and private debts is to stop having all our money created as debt. It's a 'no-brainer'. So why don't we get them to stop it?

---

29. Like the Bank of England in the UK, the Fed in the USA, and the European Central Bank in the eurozone.

CHAPTER 4

Collecting and spending public revenue

Controlling the *collection of public revenue* and its *spending for public purposes* are the second and third primary money functions of governments, as described in the Introduction to Part 2. The first function is controlling how the *money supply* is created and managed (Chapter 3), and the fourth and fifth are controlling the *borrowing of money* for public purposes and *regulating* private-sector financial activities. In the UK the Treasury is responsible for supervising all these five government functions.

The fourth and fifth – *borrowing money* for public purposes and *regulating* private-sector financial activities – are needed to correct failings in how the first three functions work. The reforms proposed to modernise the first three should therefore reduce, and ideally remove altogether, the need for the fourth and fifth. This is not yet generally understood. It is easier to understand it when you remember why the Bank of England was set up in 1694[1] and why, at the present time, increasingly complex regulations are needed to control how private banking corporations exercise the privilege of creating the national money supply at profit to themselves.

Only connect: the need to understand the links

In the UK, the Revenue & Customs collect most of the *public revenue* as taxes and charges, according to policies supervised by the Treasury. Each of the 22 present *spending* departments of central government – alphabetically from the Attorney-General's Office to the Wales Office – is responsible for what it spends under the Treasury's supervision.

---

1. See the section in Chapter 1 on 'The Bank of England: the first central bank' (p. 54).

The Introduction to this book mentioned a topical example of the Treasury's failure to co-ordinate the second and third functions – public revenue collection and public spending. The personal taxes that transfer money from citizens to the state (revenue collection) and the personal benefits and tax credits that transfer money from the state to citizens (public spending) have evolved piecemeal over the years more or less separately from each other. The result now is that the present UK government has found it difficult to bring them together to reflect the mutual financial responsibilities between citizens and society, in ways that are understandable to citizens and the civil servants who have to deal with them on society's behalf.[2]

The unrealised potential for achieving that and other synergies between the first three money functions of national governments is very great. Some examples are given later in this chapter.

Realising them will result from combining:

- necessary reform of the present inefficient and unjust arrangements for creating and managing the national money supply (described in Chapter 3) – which, unreformed, now favour the rich over the poor, together with
- necessary reform of the present inefficient and unjust arrangements for taxing what is now taxed instead of what should be taxed – which also now favour the rich over the poor (described next in this chapter), and together with
- a necessary shift in public spending which includes providing a universal Citizen's Income (basic income) as a fair share of the annual value of common resources (described later in this chapter).

Combining those reforms will greatly reduce the need for the additions to governmental services and expenditures which were developed during the 20th century to provide necessary social welfare, and the new ones which are being developed now to encourage environmental sustainability. Those special-purpose social and environmental government expenditures are needed now to compensate for how our mainstream money system – based on the three main functions of providing the national money supply, collecting public revenue and spending it on public purposes – has failed to keep up with the changing needs of the times, as follows.

---

2. On another similar point, it was only in 2005 that the two revenue departments, the Inland Revenue and the Customs & Excise, were merged as HM Revenue & Customs, enabling the UK government to develop a better integrated approach to different forms of taxation – if elected UK ministers should ever accept the need for one.

Tax avoidance/evasion, false benefit claims, and 'moral hazard'

Technically, 'tax avoidance' refers to finding loopholes in the existing laws that make it permissible to reduce the total amount of tax you would otherwise have to pay, whereas 'tax evasion' involves criminal disregard for the laws. In practice it is often difficult to be sure where the boundary lies between legally permissible 'avoidance' activities and criminal 'evasion' ones.

So tax avoidance appeals to people and businesses rich enough to afford the advice of expensive lawyers and bankers to help them to avoid paying large sums of money they would otherwise have to pay in tax. To compare it with benefit fraud, UK benefit fraud costs taxpayers an estimated £1bn a year, while the total cost of tax dodging is unknown (thanks to secretive tax havens), but is estimated to cost other UK taxpayers between £35bn and £40bn a year.[3]

The present UK government has tended to give the impression that it thinks 'benefit cheats' who make false claims for benefits at the expense of taxpayers, and the officials who inefficiently allow them to do so, are more blameworthy than 'tax cheats' who avoid paying their due taxes at the expense of other taxpayers, and the officials who inefficiently allow them to do so. That comparison matches the way the recent scandal of MPs' expenses, blameworthy as it was, distracted attention from the massively greater scale of the financial and social damage done to us all, and still being suffered, by giving the commercial banks the privilege of creating 97% of the national money supply as interest-bearing debt to themselves.

Straining at gnats, while swallowing camels? Yes. But we must also recognise that benefit cheating, tax cheating, and the continuing cheating of the rest of society by commercial banks, are all examples of the 'moral hazard'[4] that every branch of the money system offers to its practitioners as it becomes increasingly complicated and difficult for the majority of people to understand.

---

3. See, for example, http://tinyurl.com/7dfy84s, http://tinyurl.com/6wo30xj and http://tinyurl.com/8x9zcsy. Thanks to Steve Kurtz for these references. 4. 'Moral hazard' is often used to describe subsidised risk-taking that will create unlimited private profit as the reward for success for the risk-takers while limiting their losses at public expense. Banks being 'too big to fail' is a good example. 'Moral hazard' can also be used more widely to describe any situation where the risk-takers take profit from success but other parties to a transaction bear most of any losses.

Reforms needed – a summary
1. Reform of the present inefficient and unjust arrangements for creating and managing the national money supply (described in Chapter 3) – which, unreformed, now favour the rich against the poor.
2. Reform of the present inefficient and unjust arrangements for taxing what is now taxed instead of what should be taxed – which also now favour the rich against the poor.
3. A necessary shift in public spending which includes providing a universal Citizen's Income (basic income) as a fair share of the annual value of common resources.

Raising national public revenue: the need for a tax shift

Existing taxes are increasingly out of tune with the times. For example:

- Conventional national leaders in a *competitive global economy* feel pressed to reduce taxes on incomes, profits and capital in order to attract investment capital and highly qualified people.
- In *ageing societies* it is steadily becoming more difficult to meet the needs of the growing proportion of economically inactive people by taxing the work and enterprise of the declining proportion of people of working age.
- The values of assets like land and housing that mostly belong to *older and richer* owners are now largely untaxed, while the rewards earned by *younger and less rich* people from work and enterprise are taxed significantly. If that continues, it will continue in the long-term to raise the prices of houses faster than the value of wages and salaries – making it increasingly difficult for younger and poorer people to get on to the housing ladder, and widening the wealth gaps between richer and poorer people, and between older and younger ones. Those outcomes seriously threaten our future economic, social and political stability, and their combination could prove very damaging.
- *Internet trading* will continue to make it more difficult for governments to collect customs duties, value added tax and other taxes and levies on sales, and easier for companies and rich individuals to shift their earnings and profits to low-tax regimes and tax havens.
- *Tax avoidance* by big corporations and rich individuals has increased hugely in recent years. The Tax Justice Movement has estimated that tax havens cost governments worldwide £250bn annually in lost taxes; and

that tax havens hold assets of $11.5 trillion ($11,500bn), seriously distorting economic priorities, and encouraging criminal money laundering. Estimates for 2007 suggested that cross-border flows of money from criminal activities, corruption, and tax avoidance and evasion amounted to $1-1.6 *trillion* per year. Much of that total ended up with rich individuals and businesses in rich countries at the expense of the peoples and governments of poorer countries.[5]

Although some steps are apparently now being taken to penalise rich British taxpayers who have been using tax havens to avoid paying their due taxes,[6] significant reduction in the scale of tax avoidance and tax evasion may eventually prove to depend on shifting taxes off money incomes and capital that can be moved to low-tax jurisdictions, and on to the value of land and other environmental resources that cannot be moved from one tax jurisdiction to another.

Why the existing tax system is not working
1. Pressure on conventional national leaders in a competitive global economy to reduce taxes on incomes, profits and capital in order to attract investment capital and highly qualified people.
2. The difficulty in ageing societies to meet the needs of the growing proportion of economically inactive people by taxing the work and enterprise of the declining proportion of people of working age.
3. The values of assets like land and housing that mostly belong to older and richer owners are now largely untaxed, while the rewards earned by younger and less rich people from work and enterprise are taxed significantly.
4. Internet trading will continue to make it more difficult for governments to collect customs duties, value added tax and other taxes and levies on sales, and easier for companies and rich individuals to shift their earnings and profits to low-tax regimes and tax havens.
5. Tax avoidance by big corporations and rich individuals has already increased hugely in recent years. This primarily benefits rich individuals and businesses in rich countries at the expense of the peoples and governments of poorer countries.

Existing taxes are not just threatened by the prospect of inadequacy; they are positively perverse:

5. See http://tinyurl.com/ykqodjt. 6. www.express.co.uk/posts/view/266993.

- Heavily taxing employment and rewards for work and enterprise – by income tax, national insurance, profits tax and value added tax (VAT) – combined with lightly taxing the use of common resources, systematically encourages the under-use and under-development of human resources of knowledge, capability and skills, and the over-use of essential planetary resources, such as energy and the environment's capacity to absorb pollution, including carbon emissions.
- Similarly, as mentioned above, taxing the value added by the majority of people's positive contributions to society and failing to tax the value subtracted by the better-off minority who most benefit from the rising value of common resources like land, unjustly skews the overall tax burden in favour of richer against poorer people.

These points all confirm the need for a shift of taxes *off* activities that contribute to common wealth and well-being, and *on to* taxes on activities that subtract value from common resources and divert it to private profit and benefit.

Common resources

Common resources are resources whose value is due to nature or the activities and demands of society as a whole, and not to the efforts or skill of the people or organisations owning them or otherwise having exclusive access to them.

The principles underlying all the reforms of the money system proposed in this book are that governments representing the public interest should make people and organisations pay for the value they take from common resources for their own benefit; and that, while governments should continue to spend some of that money on providing services and other projects in the public interest, they should distribute the rest as a Citizen's Income. That will be for all citizens to spend personally to meet their own needs and the needs of other people – as a practical step towards a genuine version of a Big Society as floated by Prime Minister David Cameron.

The shift to a Citizen's Income can be seen as an economically relevant predistributive approach, in contrast to the conventional redistributive approach to the use of public money to meet social needs as if those are quite separate from economic purposes. The balance at any time between the amount of public revenue spent on public services and projects and the amount distributed as a Citizen's Income will be democratically decided by governments under parliamentary budgeting procedures.

Chapter 3 has shown why and how the value arising from creating the public money supply, a vital common resource, should be captured as public revenue and no longer as private profit. The value of land is probably the next most obvious common resource.

The value of land-sites, leaving aside the value of what their owners may have built on them, is almost wholly due to their location, the activities and plans of other people and businesses in them and around them, and the resulting demand for them – and in some cases due to natural features of the land such as soil fertility. In practice, many increases in land values are directly due to public investment in infrastructure – roads, railways, hospitals, schools, and so on – in and around the area. Without land value taxation, the public money invested in those public projects turns into unearned profit to the landowners passively benefiting from it.[7]

A well-publicised illustration of this in the UK was that, after the London Underground Jubilee Line extension was opened in 1999, the value of properties in the areas served by stations along its route rose by an estimated total of £13bn. Access to them was going to be much improved. Announcement of a public policy decision followed by investment of public money gave the owners of those properties a huge windfall financial gain. They had done nothing and paid nothing for it; it was a very large free lunch.[8]

By contrast, the Treasury's auction in 2000 of twenty-year licences to use the radio spectrum for the third generation of mobile phones raised £22.5bn for UK taxpayers, and governments of other European countries raised significant revenue that way too.[9]

In addition to those mentioned so far – the national money supply (in Chapter 3), land-sites, and the electromagnetic spectrum – the biggest category of common resources includes the environment's many natural resources like energy, water, soil fertility, the limited space available for road traffic and airport landing slots, and – by no means least important – the limited capacity of the environment to absorb pollution and waste, including carbon emis-

---

7. Fred Harrison's *The Power in the Land* and other books are a prime source of information and comment on the wide-ranging arguments for land value tax (LVT). See http://tinyurl.com/78hbzq5.
8. See (1) 'Land campaign – Why we should follow Pittsburgh', Christopher Huhne (later a Cabinet Minister in the UK Coalition Government of 2010), *New Statesman*, 27 September 2004. http://tinyurl.com/7adobfs. (2) Samuel Brittan, 'A case for taxing land', *Financial Times*, 9 December 2005. http://tinyurl.com/76x9hpc. 9. http://tinyurl.com/yjgdmyv.

sions. The total annual money value subtracted for private profit by whoever uses these common resources untaxed grows in step with economic growth.[10] Collecting it as public revenue in the form of taxes and charges will reduce the need for many existing taxes, including taxes on incomes, profits, and value added (VAT).

National public spending: the need for a shift in spending

One of the main positive shifts in national public spending must be to include the provision of a universal Citizen's Income payable to all citizens as a right. It will cover state pensions, child allowances, and many other existing social benefits, tax allowances, tax reliefs and tax credits.[11]

It will recognise that responsible citizens in a democratic society have a right to share a significant part of the public revenue from the value of common resources. It will *enable* people to become less dependent for welfare and work on big government, big business, big finance and foreign trade. Because all of those incur environmentally wasteful overhead costs, it will also have a *conserving* effect.[12]

It may be objected that many irresponsible people at both ends of the social spectrum – richest and poorest – will take advantage of a Citizen's Income to make no useful contribution to society. It will be necessary to correct the danger of that possible effect, at the rich end of the spectrum by closing off the present opportunities for avoiding payment of due taxes, and at the poorer end by providing wide ranges of better social, economic and cultural opportunities for a socially useful life, and sharper deterrents against anti-social behaviour. In order to be effective, the necessary action – especially at the poorer end of the spectrum – will have to go forward against a much more genuine background of social and economic justice than exists today.

---

10. Among a very large number of sources of information on environmental taxes like these, a Google Search for 'Paul Ekins & David Gee' would be a good place to start browsing. It will include www.greenfiscalcommission.org.uk. 11. See www.citizensincome.org – also search that site for 'basic income'. A Citizen's Income will play an essential part in the transition to a meaningful 'Big Society', even if people in big government, big business, big trade unions, and big banking and finance resent their resulting loss of power over other people. 12. Their present environmentally wasteful costs include duplication of buildings, heating, lighting, etc. between homes and 'workplaces', the costs of daily mass commuting to and from those, and the costs of mass transportation involved in foreign trade.

(The issue of a Citizen's Income is relevant to questions about the aims of our spending on overseas aid and its aims as part of the international money system discussed in Chapter 5. It does *not* imply that our aid to other countries should contribute directly to universal Citizen's Incomes there. But it does suggest that our aid should help them to become more self-reliant in meeting their own needs, and not more dependent on trade with richer nations on disadvantageous terms.)

The cost of a national Citizen's Income could be directly covered by distributing revenue raised by taxing private profits from the use of common resources, plus savings from the pensions, allowances, social benefits, etc. that the Citizen's Income replaced.[13]

If government and parliament decide to raise a Citizen's Income to a higher level than that, the necessary additional money could come from four main reductions in other existing spending:

(1) on interest on government debt,
(2) on perverse subsidies,
(3) on costly contracts to private sector business and finance for providing dependency-reinforcing public facilities and services,[14] and
(4) on other wasteful public spending.

First, UK government debt. The £1 trillion (£1,000,000,000,000) total having been reached in January 2012, this now incurs an annual interest cost of £43bn. Even then, as the Taxpayer's Alliance pointed out in 'The Real National Debt' (Research Note 78 of 19 October 2010), those figures do not include items such as Private Finance Initiatives (PFI); the real total is probably nearer £8 trillion.[15] The only reason why these total debts and the interest payments on them may have to stay at these absurdly high levels is our self-inflicted dependence on the commercial banks to provide our money supply as interest-bearing debt. Once we have got rid of that burden, a good deal more than the present annual interest cost of £43bn will become available for other public purposes, as Chapter 3 made clear.

13. A fuller account of this approach for anyone wanting to go further into it is at www.jamesrobertson.com/ne/benefitsandtaxes-1994.pdf. The statistics in it are now out of date. Otherwise it is still as relevant as it was when it was written. 14. These include costs of £82bn a year (2009) for 'outsourced' public services (Oxford Economics for Business Services Association – see www.bsa-org.com/documents/70 and text under Chart 2.1. 15. http://tinyurl.com/76c847x and www.taxpayersalliance.com – search for 'real debt').

Second, perverse subsidies. Upwards of US$2 trillion a year is now spent worldwide on *perverse subsidies* to economically, socially and environmentally damaging activities.[16] These include the subsidies from rich-country governments to their farming and agricultural sectors, which – combined with pressure on developing countries to open their markets to cheap food imports – have devastated those sectors in poorer countries. Many other perverse subsidies need to be eliminated, including those that finance fossil-fuel energy extraction and use, ecologically damaging road building and transport, water pollution and waste, fisheries over-exploitation, and excessive environmental destruction of forests and by mining.[17]

Third, contracts to the private sector. Politicians and government officials in recent years have incurred huge costs for contracts to private-sector business and finance to provide expensive public facilities and services. The most notorious examples in recent years have been under the Private Finance Initiative of Conservative and Labour governments. The government debt they incurred under it has largely been 'off balance sheet', Enron-style. But figures published in November 2010 showed the outstanding total government debt for PFI contracts had risen to £267 billion.[18]

Much of the money now spent under this third category of public spending would be better used if it were distributed directly to citizens as a Citizen's Income. It would give us more power of control over how the money is spent and invested, and of deciding how we will work to meet our own local needs and priorities and those of our families and neighbours. Today we have to depend on remotely controlled big business, big finance and big government to make those decisions for us. Much more could, of course, be saved from what the government now spends on the banks, if the national money supply from money created by them as debt was converted into debt-free money created by the central bank and put into circulation as public spending by the government.[19]

16. This does not include the huge present subsidy to the commercial banks (Chapter 3). 17. Norman Myers, *Perverse Subsidies: Tax $s Undercutting Our Economies and Environments Alike*, IISD, Winnipeg, Canada, 1998. 18. See http://tinyurl.com/4hh8e97, also George Monbiot at http://tinyurl.com/6mgahbq, and see also http://tinyurl.com/4mbhpgh. 19. *The Daily Telegraph*, 18 February 2011, http://tinyurl.com/4x7jalw.

Fourth, eliminating inefficiency, duplication and waste may sound an unexciting way to help to save the world. But it is important and there will continue to be plenty of scope for it in the public sector – and in the private sector too. A modernised Treasury must learn to take a 'whole-systems' approach to identifying potential synergies between the different money functions of the government and advising elected ministers how to realise them.

The four areas for reducing public expenditure
1. Interest on public debt and other government expenditure like Private Finance Initiative projects.
2. Perverse subsidies on economically, socially and environmentally damaging activities, like the subsidies to the farming and agricultural sectors in rich countries and subsidies paid for fossil-fuel extraction and use, mining and forestry destruction.
3. Contracts to the private sector for the provision of expensive public facilities and services.
4. The elimination of inefficiency, duplication and waste by developing synergies between the different money functions of government (see table on page 137).

Potential synergies

Here are some examples of synergies that will arise from linking the changes needed in how the money supply is created and managed (Chapter 3) and how public revenue is raised and public money is spent (this chapter). Although they do not imply that one desirable reform depends on another being carried out, they make it clear that the separate reforms would fit well together as parts of a coherent reform of the money system as a whole.

Synergy (1): Tax shift to land value taxation + monetary reform = stable and affordable house prices.

The failure to tax land values while taxing earnings and profits from useful work and enterprise, combined with allowing banks, as at present, to create money and direct its first use into loans for investment in existing houses and the land they occupy, creates a long-term self-reinforcing upward spiral in land values. That is because it increases their collateral value for further loans to invest in the same houses and land.

This self-reinforcing spiral results in long-term house-price booms based on speculative investment in the value of already existing assets, regularly punctuated by busts in housing values. Those busts particularly damage householders who are hit by 'negative equity', when the market value of their houses falls below their outstanding mortgage debt. The systematic long-term effect of these house-price busts is, believe it or not, the same as that of the house-price booms – a widening gap between rich and poor.[20]

The two causes of that damaging economic distortion will be removed by combining tax reform with monetary reform as described above. Both those reforms will jointly help to smooth out the peaks and troughs of economic cycles now caused by house-price booms and busts and banking booms and busts. When land values are taxed, continual rises in the capital value of land will be reduced, with the result that the banks will no longer be so keen to stoke up the spiral by offering bigger and bigger loans for land and housing purchases at higher and higher prices; and, when banks are no longer allowed to create new money, they will no longer be able to direct money into speculative investment in rising land and house prices on its first entry into circulation.

So far as economic efficiency is concerned, both reforms will remove taxes and charges on people that now distort the economy. At the outset, monetary reform will replace all of the non-cash money in circulation with debt-free money as described earlier. Meanwhile, the tax shift will replace taxes that now damage the efficiency of the economy with taxes that, by using the society-created value of land and other environmental resources for the common benefit instead of for subsidised private profit, will improve economic efficiency.

So far as fairness is concerned, both monetary reform and the tax shift will distribute more fairly the publicly created value of resources that should be shared in common, and remove the unearned 'free lunches' now enjoyed by landowners, bankers and financiers, business corporations and better-off

---

20. How much the gap is steadily widening is suggested by the example which I quoted in another context in Chapter 2. Over the longer term, the rate of increase in the price of houses has hugely eclipsed increases in the prices of other products and people's earnings. A particular house in Chelsea in London was sold for £1,000 in 1910; ninety years later it was worth £4.5 million, an increase of 450,000%, nearly 37 times greater than the increase in the price of a basket of basic items like bread and potatoes over the same period. Fred Harrison, *Boom/Bust: House Prices, Banking and the Depression of 2010*, page 117: Shepheard-Walwyn, London, 2005, one of Fred Harrison's many pioneering books on the need for Land Value Taxation.

people who are now allowed to enclose the value of those common resources for private profit.[21]

Both reforms will also open up opportunities for enterprise and work for people who are now excluded from them; discourage environmentally damaging activities; and help to make the monetary system and the tax system more transparent – in other words, allow citizens, politicians, economists, and other concerned professionals to understand how they work and how their working might be improved.

But what about supply and demand? There is still the fact that Mark Twain noted: "Buy land. They're not making any more." Competition between a limited supply of desirable houses and a potentially unlimited demand for them may keep the value of land and housing rising higher and faster than other things, even if monetary reform and a shift in taxes help to limit the financial demand for them.

There is no need to dispute that possibility. But it is irrelevant to the need to remove the unnecessarily damaging features of how we allow the money system to work now. It is also a further reason, if one is necessary, for supporting a Citizen's Income to limit the impact of widening the rich-poor gap.

Support for each of these proposed reforms – monetary reform and tax shift – has been growing noticeably in recent years, but separately among two different sets of activists, politicians, academics and professionals. The two approaches clearly support each other and the common interest. So it was a pity that past supporters of the two tended to compete over their relative importance and priority. It is encouraging that they are beginning to recognise it as a case of 'both . . . and', not 'either . . . or'.[22]

(2) Monetary reform + tax shift + public spending shift = Citizen's Income.

The conventional assumption has been that there is no way of funding a Citizen's Income except by taxing people's other incomes highly, and it might have to be at a rate as high as 70%. For many years that has been seen as

---

21. For free lunches see www.the-free-lunch.blogspot.com. Land enclosure has played a prominent part in widening the gap between rich and poor in the history of 'developed' economies and continues to play that part in 'emerging' economies today. See, for a recent example, http://tinyurl.com/727j93t. 22. Alanna Hartzok is one: see www.earthrights.net. Appendix 1 provides background to the Georgist and Social Credit movements.

ruling out a Citizen's Income. Like many objections to otherwise desirable proposals, the assumption is due to inability or unwillingness to think outside a narrow box.

There is actually no problem. The extra money needed on top of what is now spent on the pensions, allowances, benefits, tax reliefs and tax credits that a Citizen's Income will replace can easily be found from within the three sources above – new revenue from monetary reform, taxing values subtracted from common resources, and savings from existing spending.

(3) Monetary reform + Citizen's Income = financial stability.

The recent 'credit' boom and 'credit' famine that has followed it were caused by allowing commercial banks to create the money supply as profit-making debt. They naturally created much too much money in the boom and then much too little in the famine.

As an emergency measure the Bank of England has exercised the power of 'quantitative easing' – jargon for central banks themselves creating billions of new money and, in effect, giving them to commercial banks to circulate into the economy. In practice, that channel for injecting emergency money into circulation has not worked very well. It is turning out to have stimulated inflation without economic recovery; and, so far as the commercial banks are concerned, it has seemed temporarily to confirm their complacent assumption that, one way or another, for the foreseeable future, our government would continue to condemn us to depend on them for providing our money supply.

However, it may not be long now before public opinion becomes powerful enough to insist that full-blown monetary reform is implemented. In due course it should show that the Bank of England, by itself creating or withdrawing the right amounts of money from circulation, can keep the money supply at the required level. But, if emergencies should then happen from time to time, and if arrangements already exist for distributing a Citizen's Income, the quickest and fairest way of injecting new emergency money into every part of the economy – besides also directly benefiting the people who most need support in difficult economic times – will be a temporary increase in the amount of money put into circulation as a Citizen's Income.

No longer will the commercial banking system be seen as the well paid gatekeeper necessarily controlling where almost all new money goes on entering the economy.

Developing synergies between the different money functions of government
Synergy (1): Tax shift to land value taxation + monetary reform = stable and affordable house prices
• the failure to tax land values combined with allowing banks to create money and direct its first use into the property market creates a long-term self-reinforcing upward spiral in land values. • the tax shift will move taxes off rewards (earnings and profits) for work and enterprise and on to taxes on activities that subtract values from common resources like land and other environmental resources. • the monetary reform will involve the creation of debt-free money created by the central bank and given to the elected government as public revenue to spend into circulation in the public interest. • both those reforms will jointly help to smooth out the peaks and troughs of economic cycles now caused by house-price booms and busts, and banking booms and busts.
Synergy (2): Monetary reform + tax shift + public spending shift = Citizen's Income
• the extra money needed to fund a Citizen's Income in addition to what is now spent on state pensions, allowances, benefits, tax reliefs and tax credits, can easily be found from new revenue from monetary reform, taxing values subtracted from common resources, and savings from existing spending.
Synergy (3): Monetary reform + Citizen's Income = financial stability
• the current monetary system leads to credit 'booms' and credit 'famines'. • the money system would become more stable if the Bank of England was given power itself to create the right amounts of money into circulation or withdraw it from circulation. • the quickest and fairest way of injecting new emergency money into every part of the economy will be a temporary increase in the amount of money put into circulation as a Citizen's Income.

Looking further ahead

Chapter 13 of my earlier book *Future Wealth*, published in 1989 (23 years ago) posed the following question:[23] "How should we set about applying the principles of the new economic order to specific spheres of real economic activity and real life? This chapter briefly outlines the strategic reappraisals needed for:

23. www.jamesrobertson.com/book/futurewealth-section3.pdf.

- work;
- technology and industry;
- energy;
- food and agriculture;
- transport, housing and planning;
- health;
- information and communication;
- education, leisure and the arts; and
- peace, order and security . . .

In each of these spheres and others like them the principles and the implications of an enabling and conserving economy need to be worked out in a systematic way . . . "

No government has yet seriously undertaken that task, but as it becomes more clearly urgent, the need for further shifts in the patterns of public spending aiming to *enable and conserve* will be evident.

They will give higher priority than at present to new ways of encouraging positive things like peace, a socially responsible and mutually supportive society, good health and good work (not only by employees for employers). That will contrast with the higher priority now given to developing new technologies, weapons and practices to deal with negative things like war, crime, disease and unemployment when they happen.

One of the main obstacles to this desirable shift from negative to positive priorities is that the development of new weapons, technologies and practices accepting and responding to future war, crime, sickness and disease are more obviously profitable in money values than new ways of preventing those things happening at all. They therefore make a bigger contribution to money-measured economic growth. So, according to today's conventional economic understanding, policy makers give them higher priority than they give to efforts to create a better world.

Assuming that it becomes generally accepted quite soon that reliance on money-measured economic growth in its present form is a disastrously misleading basis for policy decisions, further shifts in many fields of government spending, including those shown in the following table, may become possible and necessary.

Some typical fields of public spending (£bn 2011)	
Health Care	£121.2
Education	£33.2
Defence	£45.6
Welfare	£58.7
Debt interest	£43.7
TOTAL (including other spending areas)	£512.2 [24]

The fourth and fifth Treasury functions

The modernising reforms proposed for the first three Treasury functions – providing the national money supply, collecting public revenue, and spending it on public purposes – should reduce and almost entirely remove the need for the fourth and fifth – borrowing money for public purposes and regulating private sector financial activities.

Governments' borrowing needs. A well-managed, reformed money system will reduce governments' borrowing needs to those required for supporting 'work in progress' – to finance seasonal variations between public revenue coming in and public spending going out.

National Savings and Investments (NS&I) in the UK has almost £100bn invested in it by the public; it is guaranteed by the Treasury; and its purpose is to provide cost-effective lending to the government.[25] After money system reform, there should be no need for more government borrowing than that.

Regulating private sector financial activities. Today the very heavy and costly burdens of financial regulation by central banks, and by agencies like the Financial Services Authority in the UK and its counterparts elsewhere, are almost entirely needed to deal with problems arising from allowing commercial banks to create the world's money as profit-making debt. Once that has been phased out as proposed in Chapter 3, special regulation of private sector financial enterprises should no longer be needed.[26]

---

24. The figures are taken from: http://tinyurl.com/6vodry6. 25. http://tinyurl.com/85hswrn.
26. See the Section on Regulation, Supervision and Guarantees in Chapter 3 and footnote 24 there, comparing the present need for these complicated regulations to the epicycles piled on epicycles that were needed to correct the errors of pre-Copernican astronomy.

Proposals from Chapters 3 and 4

The reforms proposed in these two chapters are summarised in the table below. That set of reforms will transform the national money system into one much better organised than at present to serve its purposes in the 21st century. We should think of it as a shift from redistribution that aims to correct the outcomes of a badly organised and managed money system, to predistribution that organises a money system better designed to meet its purposes.

It will also provide a model for the functions of the *international money system*, designed to meet the needs of world society today and in the future – see Chapter 5.

Finally, it will provide an enabling, no longer a disabling, context for the development of *local money systems* and their revival in more self-reliant local economies – Chapter 6.

Reforms proposed in Chapters 3 and 4 – a summary
1. Provide the national money supply as a public service
Stop the creation of money by commercial banks as profit-making debt and transfer responsibility to the central bank for creating money debt-free and giving it as public revenue to the elected government.
2. Develop other sources of revenue; shift taxes off 'goods' onto 'bads'
(a) Reduce and eventually abolish taxes on value added, incomes and profits, which penalise useful work and enterprise. (b) Replace those with taxes or charges on things and activities that subtract value from common resources. These will include taxes or charges on land-rent values and on the use or right to use other common (mainly environmental) resources and take into account the capacity of the environment to absorb pollution and waste.
3. Create a people-centred shift in public spending
Introduce a Citizen's Income – a tax-free income paid to every man, woman and child as a right of citizenship. The additional costs will be met by reducing the costs of interest on government debt, of perverse subsidies, of contracting out the provision of public infrastructure and services to the commercial business and financial sector, and of public sector inefficiency and waste.

CHAPTER 5

The international money system: what can we do about It?

The context

Recent developments have created the need for change in how the international money system now works, and increased the likelihood that change will actually happen.

First, the period of history may be coming to an end in which a single world superpower and its currency – Britain in the 19th century and the United States in the 20th – have dominated and controlled the international money system, mainly with the purpose and effect of serving the superpower's own interests. The international money system may now be about to become more democratically controlled and managed in the interest of all the peoples of the world.

Signs of this possibility during the past few years have included the former Groups of Seven countries (G7) and then Eight (G8) being largely replaced by the Group of Twenty (G20), as the body supervising global financial affairs; and serious proposals being made, though not in the end accepted, that the new head of the IMF should be from somewhere other than Europe or the United States after the resignation of Dominique Strauss-Kahn in May 2011.

Alternative, but less democratic and less desirable, developments would be for the USA to be replaced:

- either by China as the world's emerging superpower, with the Chinese yuan (renminbi) taking the place of the US dollar as the dominant currency for international transactions,[1]

- or by an unrepresentative oligarchy of major currencies – such as the US dollar, Chinese yuan, European euro, Japanese yen, Russian rouble and British pound sterling – competing with one another to provide the *de facto* world currency.

Second, on the other hand, increasing globalisation of the world economy since the Second World War, and the growing power of transnational businesses and banks and other financial corporations – outside national control but supported by a largely unreformed IMF and World Bank – raises further questions about the purposes of the international money system and its control.

Third, and fundamentally most important and urgent, is the growing ecological threat to human civilisation and our need to deal with it globally, as well as nationally and locally.[2] The whole range of interconnected systems that enables us to rely on the planet's resources for our well-being and survival is being increasingly stressed, at least partly by how the growing world population aspires to live.

We may now be approaching what has been called 'Peak Everything'.[3] That is the point at which the availability of all the Earth's resources most important to us – such as sustainable sources of usable energy, necessary food and drinkable water – may begin to decline; the decline of each may then accelerate the decline of others; that may create severe scarcities that lead to breakdown of national and international law and order; and the result could be a combined worldwide collapse of the social and ecological support systems that we now take for granted.

Recent developments in the world monetary system
1. The coming end to a period of history when a single world superpower and its currency have dominated and controlled the international money system. This could lead to the international monetary system becoming more democratically controlled or to less desirable alternatives.
2. The increasing globalisation of the world economy since the Second World War, and the growing power of transnational businesses and banks and other financial corporations – outside national control but supported by a largely unreformed IMF and World Bank.
3. The growing ecological threat to human civilisation and our need to deal with it globally, as well as nationally and locally.

1. www.bbc.co.uk/news/10413076. 2. http://tinyurl.com/3vzad2u. 3. http://tinyurl.com/7skqbzu.

So we have to make the money system work internationally for the same new purposes as earlier chapters have suggested for national money systems – namely:

- to enable the great majority of the world's people to meet their own needs and the needs of their families and neighbours better than most of us can today;
- to motivate us all to live in ways that will conserve and restore the resources of the planet on which we depend for our survival and well-being, instead of destroying them; and
- to distribute the value of those resources more widely and fairly among all.

New purposes for the international monetary system
1. To enable the great majority of the world's people to meet our own needs and the needs of our families and neighbours better than most of us can today.
2. To motivate us all to live in ways that will conserve and restore the resources of the planet on which we depend for our survival and well-being, instead of destroying them.
3. To distribute their value more widely and fairly among all.

At this point we should note a special complication that has arisen in the past fifteen years or so. It is exemplified by the Kyoto Protocol of 1997, and now includes various rationing schemes known as 'cap and trade', 'cap and share', 'quota trading', etc.

The effectiveness of these schemes is very much in doubt. As noted in the Introduction, practical experience of their performance to date suggests that some, like the EU Carbon Emissions Trading Scheme, have given sizeable windfall profits to heavily polluting companies, and that others too are no more than scams. Ration trading schemes of this nature are further discussed later in this chapter and again in Chapter 7. I know that many good people promote and support them with the best of intentions, but that profit-making financial entrepreneurs and corporations get them set up to make profit for themselves.

Moreover, the argument for these schemes rests on two questionable assumptions – first, that climate change is outstandingly the most important ecological threat we face and, second, that the environment's capacity to absorb carbon emissions is the only environmental resource to which the principle of contraction and convergence (whereby global usage of a resource is reduced and at the same time per capita usage of the resource becomes more equal) needs to be applied.

The International Commission on Global Governance

Sixteen years ago the Independent International Commission on Global Governance[4] published recommendations on how the international money system should "service the needs of the global neighbourhood". They broadly reflected the three aims of:

- modernising how the *international money supply* is created and managed;
- developing *international revenue collection* by taxing and charging nations for the use of global commons, including ocean fishing, sea-bed mining, sea lanes, flight lanes, outer space and the electromagnetic spectrum, and for activities that pollute and damage the global environment, or cause hazards beyond national boundaries, such as emissions of CO_2 and CFCs, oil spills, and dumping wastes at sea; and
- *international spending,* financed by those taxes and charges, to meet the costs of the expanding activities of the United Nations and its organisations, including international disaster relief and peacekeeping.[5]

A development of the international money system along those lines, including global monetary reform, taxing and charging, and spending on public purposes:

- would encourage environmentally sustainable development worldwide;
- would provide a much needed source of revenue for the United Nations;
- would provide substantial financial transfers to developing countries by right and without strings, as compensation for rich countries' disproportionate use of world resources in the past;
- would help to liberate developing countries from dependence on grants and loans from institutions like the World Bank and International Monetary Fund;

---

4. *Our Global Neighbourhood*, Oxford University Press, 1995. 5. Revenue from global taxes might also have funded the per capita distribution of some of it to national governments, as a right of every citizen of the world to a share in the value of global resources as a global Citizen's Income, but the International Commission did not mention that.

- would help to solve the problem of Third World debt;
- would recognise the shared status of all people as citizens of the world; and
- would contribute to global security and peace by helping to reduce the sense of injustice in a globalised world.

All very sensible. But what progress has been made since then?

International monetary reform[6]

In recent years awareness of the need for international monetary reform for a globalised world economy has grown. A genuinely international currency is needed to provide the supply of money for conducting international transactions in the more democratic and conserving age that we hope we are now entering.

In the early years of this century there was growing criticism of the 'dollar hegemony' of the United States. For example, in 2002 the rest of the world was estimated to pay the US at least $400bn a year for using the dollar as the main global currency. A Pentagon analyst justified this as payment to the US for keeping world order; others saw it as enabling the richest country in the world to compel poorer ones to pay for its unsustainable consumption of global resources.[7] To build up their reserves, poor countries had to borrow dollars from the US at interest rates as high as 18% and lend it back to the US for Treasury Bonds at 3%.[8] The dollar was a global monetary instrument that the US, and only the US, could produce; world trade had become "a game in which the US produces dollars and the rest of the world produces things that dollars can buy".[9]

More recently, as mentioned already, possibilities have been mooted that the Chinese yuan (or renminbi) could eclipse the US dollar as the world's leading currency and perhaps replace it as the world's dominant 'reserve currency'; or that a number of reserve currencies might end up competing with

---

6. Michael Rowbotham, *Goodbye America! Globalisation, debt and the dollar empire*, Jon Carpenter, 2000, is a valuable international successor to his *The Grip of Death*. 7. Richard Douthwaite, *Defense and the Dollar*, 2002 and Feasta, *Climate and Currency: Proposals for Global Monetary Reform*, 2002. Details of both from The Foundation for the Economics of Sustainability, e-mail: feasta@anu.ie. 8. Romilly Greenhill and Ann Pettifor, *The United States as a HIPC* (heavily indebted prosperous country) – how the poor are financing the rich, new economics foundation, London, 2003; http://tinyurl.com/76notmt. 9. Henry C. K. Liu, 'US Dollar Hegemony Has Got To Go', Asia Times Online Co. Ltd, 2002.

one another to handle international transactions as agreed between payers and payees.

However, the strongest proposal is the one floated by the IMF in April 2010 after pressure mainly from the BRICs group of countries – Brazil, Russia, India and China. This envisages a process of step-by-step development starting with increased issues of Special Drawing Rights (SDRs) by the IMF and eventually culminating in the issue by a new World Central Bank of a genuinely international currency – called 'bancor' in memory of the world currency proposed by Keynes at the Bretton Woods conference in 1944 and rejected then by the Americans.[10]

In the IMF's view the 'bancor' might be either a common currency, like the euro, replacing the former currencies of its user countries; or it might be a parallel currency available to all countries to use for international transactions if they chose to do so, coexisting with their own national currencies for use in domestic transactions.

It is difficult to imagine it as a common currency, in the sense that it would replace existing national currencies. It should be a parallel currency, for the same reasons that in 2002 it was right for the UK to keep the pound but also use the euro as a parallel currency when it suited our interests to do so.[11] As I said then,

> "We should be prepared for the possible emergence of a worldwide pattern of coexisting parallel currencies at different levels – supranational (including global, in due course), national, and local. As a feature of world development over the coming decades, this will be in tune with the increasingly global *and* increasingly local character of 21st-century life. It will reflect a preference for an organic rather than a mechanistic, one-size-fits-all approach to monetary progress."

Meanwhile, an eminently sensible proposal has been put forward by Jakob von Uexkull of the World Future Council[12] that the IMF should issue at least $100 billion in SDRs to support the new Green Climate Fund set up under the UN under the December 2010 Cancun Agreement. (This proposal would meet the urgency of the worldwide need for investment in green

10. International Monetary Fund, *Reserve Accumulation and International Monetary Stability*, April 2013, http://tinyurl.com/2bw94yf. 11. *Forward with the euro – And the pound*, Economic Research Council, 2002. See www.jamesrobertson.com/article/forward.pdf. 12. http://tinyurl.com/869fvw7.

energy supply and conserving energy use, and not be open to the faults of the 'cap and trade' schemes discussed again later in this chapter.)

Possible opposition to international monetary reform

Apart from people who benefit financially from having the US dollar as the currency mainly used for international transactions, and people whose instinctive habit is to prefer the status quo rather than change, two other sets of people could be opposed to international monetary reform.

First, there are people who have a phobia about the prospect of one-world government and are alarmed by the idea of a world currency and a world central bank.[13] They include people who have suffered at the hands of present or recent totalitarian or corrupt governments or 'nanny states', and people who – notably in the USA – have inherited a perception of government as something imposed on them 300 years ago by an alien colonial power. Some of them would prefer to 'let a thousand flowers bloom' and risk a free-for-all that gives multi-billion dollar windfalls to profit-making mega-corporations, business oligarchs, and grossly rich individuals. Mistakenly, but perhaps understandably, they recoil from the prospect of a money system controlled by agencies serving the interests of everyone.

We have to recognise, of course, that serious corruption exists in many aspects of government activity as well as in the private sector.[14] Wherever we work, everyone is vulnerable to pressures to act in our own interest and that of our families and friends and associates. We must therefore be prevented from doing so – and be protected from those pressures – by effective safeguards of 'transparency'[15] and 'accountability'[16] that let everyone know what we have been doing and the effects it has had.

Second, in the particular case of the international money system, reforming it will call for a transformation of outlook on the part of people working in organisations like the International Monetary Fund (IMF), World Bank, Bank for International Settlements (BIS) and World Trade Organisation (WTO) –

13. That is why many of us tend to say 'governance' instead of 'government' in contexts like this. But, whatever we call it, the time has come when basic, democratic money-system functions are now needed at the global level as well as nationally. 14. It particularly exists in the 'revolving door' between the two sectors. See for example Political Cleanup, http://political-cleanup.org. Also see 'Lobbying in USA', and 'Links list' on that website. 15. www.transparency.org.uk.
16. http://tinyurl.com/7gwm8h6.

unless those are to be scrapped altogether, which doesn't seem desirable or possible.

With individual exceptions, people working in those organisations have acclimatised themselves to the 'Washington Consensus', which has dishonestly assumed that promoting improved standards of living for everyone depends on giving top priority to the interests of richer and more powerful countries, businesses and individuals. After many years of proof that this indirect 'trickle down', 'crumbs from the table' philosophy has been very damaging, those officials will now have to go into reverse, and directly serve the common interests of the majority of people and countries.[17]

Global taxes, global public spending and other global 'economic instruments'[18]

As suggested earlier in this chapter, a new overall purpose for the money system at the international level is needed on the same lines as for national money systems, namely:

- to enable the great majority of the world's people to meet their needs better than they can today,
- to motivate us all to live in ways that will conserve and restore the resources of the planet on which we depend for our survival and well-being, instead of destroying them,
- and meanwhile to distribute the value of those resources more widely and fairly.

While the need to provide and manage the international money supply by creating and managing a new genuinely international currency is reasonably easy to understand, things are much less clear when it comes to future developments on:

17. But will this actually happen? What will make it happen? The answer is that we, the people of the world, must find ways to make it happen. That applies to money system reform in general, and will be discussed further in the concluding chapter. 18. Economic instruments include taxes, charges, deposit-refunds and schemes for trading rations or quotas or permits. They are used by governmental agencies as financial incentives to encourage producers and consumers to adopt environmentally sound and efficient production and consumption. See http://tinyurl.com/7fe5kpm.

List of United Nations agencies and related organisations

Food and Agriculture Organization (FAO)
International Atomic Energy Agency (IAEA)
International Civil Aviation Organization (ICAO)
International Court of Justice (ICJ)
International Energy Association (IEA)
International Fund for Agricultural Development (IFAD)
International Labour Organization (ILO)
International Maritime Organization (IMO)
International Monetary Fund (IMF)
International Renewable Energy Agency (IRENA)
International Telecommunication Union (ITU)
UN-Habitat
UNICEF
United Nations Educational, Scientific and Cultural Organization (UNESCO)
United Nations Industrial Development Organization (UNIDO)
Universal Postal Union (UPU)
World Bank Group (WBG)
World Health Organization (WHO)
World Intellectual Property Organization (WIPO)
World Meteorological Organization (WMO)
World Tourism Organization (UNWTO)
World Trade Organization (WTO)

Note: The United Nations itself includes the:
General Assembly,
Security Council,
Economic and Social Council,
Secretariat (Secretary-General) and
Trusteeship Council

(1) global taxes to discourage undesirable international activities and to provide revenue for global public spending on global projects and programmes;
(2) necessary global public projects and programmes on which that revenue should be spent; and
(3) international 'economic instruments', such as the CO_2 emissions trading and other 'flexible mechanisms' envisaged in the Kyoto protocol, supposedly designed to bridge those two other functions but actually providing a new source of profit to privileged businesses.

We will leave the third of those on one side for the present, and ask: How should effective decisions be taken about international taxes and public spending programmes and their organisation, in order for them to meet the objectives of the wide range of UN and associated agencies shown in the box on page 149?

At this point we must accept that in recent years we, the world's people, have allowed ourselves to be distracted by the false assumption that climate change, and in that context carbon emissions, are the international ecological problem that trumps all others. Although it is hugely serious, it is not the only devastating threat we have to face.

The reality is that we face the threat of a combined collapse of the interconnected ecological systems on which human civilisation and our economic and social systems depend, for example for national and international peace and security. Most of those threats are, at least partly if not wholly, due to human activity – 'anthropogenic'. Internationally, as well as nationally and locally, we must reform the whole money system that generates the money values that motivate us all to live in the ways we now do.

The interconnected range of threats includes:

- climate change,
- shortages of food, water and energy connected with one another and also with
- distribution failures due to how the money system now works,
- poisoning of earth, water and air,
- soil erosion and loss of soil fertility,
- continuing population growth,
- deforestation,
- overfishing,

- loss of biodiversity and destruction of other species' habitats, and
- consequent breakdown of national and international peace and security.

Dealing with these questions piecemeal, without sufficient regard to the links between them, can lead to serious mistakes. An example is the subsidies to encourage the growth of biofuels to replace carbon-emitting fuels. These can have disastrous results.[19] One is the destruction of forests to clear the land to grow biofuels, ignoring the fact that forests meet a range of other ecological needs, some related directly to climate change, others for purposes like the preservation of biodiversity. Another disastrous result is the conversion of agricultural land, now growing essential food for people in poorer countries, into growing crops to produce biofuels mainly for the use of people in richer countries.

The range of interconnected environmental threats
Climate change
Shortages of food, water, and energy connected with one another and also with distribution failures due to how the money system now works
Poisoning of earth, water and air
Soil erosion and loss of soil fertility
Continuing population growth
Deforestation
Overfishing
Loss of biodiversity and destruction of other species' habitats
Consequent breakdown of national and international peace and security

So what changes will be needed at the UN level to move all those agencies (see box on page 149) toward a more effectively co-ordinated international strategy for getting the right things taxed and subsidised in the right ways, and not the wrong ones in the wrong ways?

It is quite clear that:

19. See, for example, http://tinyurl.com/7x65tja.

> "Many national strategies [for Millennium Development Goals] will require significant international support. But the international system is ill equipped to provide it because of a shortage of supportive rules, effective institutional arrangements, and above all resolve to translate commitments to action. Here we diagnose why the development system is not yet up to the task of the Millennium Development Goals (MDGs), and how it needs to scale up its financial and technical support. That system has the potential to help countries achieve the Goals, but it needs a significantly more focused approach to do so."[20]

The two references in this footnote[21] give an impression of the nature and complexity of the financial problems the UN system is now experiencing, and the responses that some of the agencies are trying to make. At least it seems that the IMF and the World Bank are trying to co-ordinate their policies more closely with those of some of the UN agencies. The World Bank's 2011 World Development Report on *Conflict, Security, and Development*[22] suggests in its 'Action Agenda' section that "what is needed is renewed commitment, in regional and global fora, on objectives and standards by which national and international actors approach peace and security, justice and inclusion, and economic governance".

That sounds well intentioned. But, in practice, what does it mean? and how can it be applied to co-ordinate the objectives of the other agencies too, and influence their financing and spending in support of the international money system's new purposes?

Pressure from active world citizens will be needed to bring a sense of urgency to the modernisation of these aspects of the international money system to meet the threats we now face. It is difficult to propose how that pressure will be most effectively asserted through the jungle of national consultative organisations like the UN Association of the UK (UNA-UK)[23] and international ones like the NGO Branch of the UN Department of Economic and Social Affairs.[24] How can we best break through the institutional inertia of that mass of relevant national and international governmental agencies? And how can we challenge the more directly focused, more heavily financed opposing pressures from global business corporations?

20. *Investing in Development: A Practical Plan to Achieve the Millennium Development Goals*, Chapter 13, p. 193, Earthscan, 2005. http://tinyurl.com/7mxbh3g. 21. See http://tinyurl.com/7hu4wpp and http://tinyurl.com/732ossg. 22. http://wdr2011.worldbank.org/agenda.
23. www.una.org.uk/about.html. 24. http://tinyurl.com/6qkkwaq.

That is not yet at all clear. People who are interested in tackling it and well placed to make progress at the international level must continue to take forward their own initiatives, and the rest of us must support them.

Meanwhile, let us not forget that there is much we should press to get done at the national level to develop more responsible new international financial relationships. One example in the UK is what is becoming known as 'the Department of Dodgy Deals', a.k.a. the Export Credits Guarantee Department (ECGD). Developing countries' debts to it amount to over £2bn, "but almost nothing is known about how these debts were created – despite many of them arising from deals with some of the world's most notorious dictators".[25]

Rationing and trading schemes versus taxes and charges

This question is about whether, and if so how, we should try to co-ordinate:

- schemes for distributing quotas or permits that ration certain activities, such as the amount of carbon that companies may emit, and then letting them sell their ration if they don't need to use all of it themselves; with
- international taxes and charges on those damaging activities.

A typical example of rationing and trading schemes is the one included in the Kyoto Protocol, based on the mechanisms of Emissions Trading (known as the carbon market), the 'Clean development mechanism', and 'Joint implementation'.[26]

The value of this and other market-based schemes is very questionable. They are mostly initiated by people in big business and their financial advisers, focused on making profit for themselves or finding 'offsets' enabling their clients to escape or reduce the need to pay for their own offending activities.

There is a balanced approach to them in *Making the Voluntary Carbon Market Work for the Poor,* Forum for the Future, 2008.[27] But readers who want to go into this more deeply, should also look at the 68-page paper *When Markets are Poison: Learning about Climate Policy from the Financial Crisis*, The Corner House, 2007.[28] It explains convincingly why the development of markets for trading rations of carbon emissions – and whatever other such

25. http://tinyurl.com/7u5x42s. 26. http://tinyurl.com/27nor2. 27. http://tinyurl.com/8a7bqc2. 28. http://tinyurl.com/6msvmhe.

activities may be proposed for rationing in future – is likely to result in an expanding new market for derivatives, such as caused the gravity of the financial collapse in 2008 from which the world still suffers.

I have already in the Introduction made a critical reference to the EU Carbon Emissions Trading Scheme and the windfall profits it has given to big heavily polluting companies.[29] Chapter 7 will include further discussion of the question of 'cap and trade' or 'cap and share' schemes, as compared with taxes and charges. It will not only confirm the probability that they will benefit big companies and those who manage them more than anyone else. It will also remind us that, by complicating how the money system works, they make it more difficult for people to understand how the whole system is intended to work, and whether or not it is working efficiently and fairly.

Conclusion

That is an appropriate note on which to end this chapter. The international money system, like the rest of the money system, has developed piecemeal in ways that make understanding how it works more and more difficult. It has become a growing jungle of activities whose purposes and the interactions between them are not at all clearly defined. Meanwhile the financial and ecological burden of its overhead administrative costs – official travel, conferences, and all the other requirements of international consultation – grows continually.

What is clear is that we need to develop the way the money system works at the international level to provide us with a genuinely international currency, and to introduce efficient systems of international taxation and public spending – and we should do so as a matter of urgency.

29. http://tinyurl.com/yjhw8mw.

CHAPTER 6

Money for localities, households and people

Economic activities have become increasingly centralised in the past 200 years, first in national economies and more recently in the global economy as well. At the same time, democracy and education have been spreading.

In the more developed economies initially, and more recently everywhere else in the world, the result has been twofold:

(1) to increase our aspirations to have more say in how we live our lives and how we are controlled; and
(2) to increase our awareness that the present way the money system works to control how we live is unsatisfactory and unjust.

Previous chapters have dealt with how we should now reform the way money works at the national and international levels. This chapter is about the effects of the proposed reforms at the level of localities, households and people's personal lives and work.

Local money systems and community currencies

Among the most interesting initiatives now taking place to modernise local activities to meet the 21st-century needs of society and the economy is the Transition Towns movement. In September 2011 over 380 communities were recognised officially as 'Transition initiatives' in the UK, Ireland, Canada, Australia, New Zealand, the USA, Italy and Chile, and there are others elsewhere too.[1] The introduction of a community currency, one

1. See http://en.wikipedia.org/wiki/Transition_Towns.

aspect of a local money system, is a key feature of a number of Transition towns.[2]

The following is often quoted as having been the original community currency. In the early 1930s, when economic activity in the Great Depression was at its lowest and unemployment was at its highest in many countries, Michael Unterguggenberger was the burgomaster in the small town of Worgl, between Salzburg and Innsbruck in Austria. He persuaded the town to issue local money as tickets ('scrip') corresponding to one, five and ten Austrian schillings. These new local banknotes were paid to unemployed people for building and repairing local streets and drains and bridges; they then spent the notes in the local shops; and the shopkeepers paid them to their local suppliers for their purchases, and back to the town as taxes.

This new currency led to a dramatic increase in local economic activity in Worgl. That was partly due to a special feature of the notes. They lost 1% of their value every month, unless their holders attached a stamp bought from the town council. People were eager to spend them as soon as possible before they lost value – which increased what economists call the 'velocity of money'; the sooner people spend it, the faster it circulates.

But the scheme was brought to a sad end. The Austrian National Bank suppressed it, fearing that successful local currencies would threaten its central control over the country's money. Many US local currencies suffered a similar fate; in 1933 the New York bankers persuaded President Roosevelt to outlaw them. We must learn from that today. It is one of many good reasons for depriving the commercial banks of the privilege of creating the national money supply as profit-making debt – as proposed in Chapter 3.

In recent years many countries have been seeing a corresponding revival of local currencies. This can now be seen as a response to a global financial and economic crisis which is as bad today as it was in the 1930s. But it must also be seen as a more permanent longer-term reaction against the steadily growing number of 'clone towns' and their financial dependence on remote organisations which are controlled somewhere else. Those include:

- remote government agencies providing people with important public services;

2. A good illustration of the close connection between the Transition Towns movement and local money systems, is at www.transitionbooks.net – see the vertical column of typical local community banknotes on the right-hand side of its home page.

- remote big businesses like supermarket chains providing local people with food and other goods; and
- remote big government or big businesses providing local people with jobs that will pay their wages.

Today's local currencies have a variety of descriptions such as 'regional', 'alternative', 'community', 'complementary', 'barter' and 'scrip'; and names like Ithaca Hours and Time Dollars in the USA, Local Exchange Trading Systems (LETS) in many English-speaking countries, the Tlaloc in Mexico, Systèmes d'Echange Locaux (SEL) in France, and Chiemgauer in Germany. (In the eurozone, the number of these currencies has grown since national currencies like the franc and the deutschmark were replaced by the more remote euro issued by the European Central Bank.)

These varieties of local currencies have generally taken the form of community currencies – that is to say that they have been set up by groups of people (or, in a few cases, groups of enterprises) to facilitate exchanging or trading with one another.[3] So far, in only a few exceptional cases have agencies of local government been supporting them. Japan provides an example.[4]

In addition to Transition communities and Rob Hopkins, noted already at footnote 1 (p. 155), the following are good personal sources of information and ideas on local currencies and local economies:

- David Boyle (UK) www.david-boyle.co.uk
- Tom Greco (USA) www.reinventingmoney.com
  (For comments on these two distinguished thinkers, see www.jamesrobertson.com/news-jun09.htm, Item 4(3)&(4) and Item 5.)
- Feasta (Ireland) www.feasta.org and www.feasta.org/documents/review2/douthwaite.htm
- David Korten and YES! Magazine (USA) www.yesmagazine.org/blogs/david-korten
- The new economics foundation (UK): search for the phrase 'Local Money', www.neweconomics.org/search/apachesolr_search/Local Money
- Ellen Laconte (USA) www.ellenlaconte.com/edge-wise
- John Rogers (UK) http://localcurrency.wordpress.com
- Bernard Lietaer www.lietaer.com
- Margrit Kennedy (Germany) www.margritkennedy.de

3. www.communitycurrency.org/cc-resources. 4. http://tinyurl.com/7qcj732.

The need for an accelerated worldwide revival of activity in local and household economies is now very urgent. In the next twenty or thirty years, local and household economies need to become significant components of national economies. A flourishing population of local money systems serving local and household economies should by then have enabled most of the world's seven billion people to become less dependent than we are at present on getting national or international money to spend on the necessities of life and to pay our taxes. Local money systems will then be recognised as parallel and complementary to the money system at national and international levels, not subordinate to them.

Reducing our present dependency on national money will be an essential aspect of achieving a new co-operative self-reliance, significantly enlarging our freedom to control our own lives in co-operation with one another. By reducing the overhead costs – ecological, social and economic – of our present over-centralised ways of organising our lives and work, it will also conserve planetary resources.[5] For example it will reduce:

- the costs of trade and traffic, and their infrastructures;
- the costs of daily commuting between homes and distant workplaces, and of duplicating the buildings, facilities and services now needed at both; and
- the continually growing overhead costs of the people who now operate, manage and regulate the continually expanding money system at national and international levels, and the people who provide them with supporting facilities and services.

Whether a sufficiently big revival of local economies with their new money systems can be accomplished quickly enough is open to question. It will largely depend on the urgency with which the reforms proposed in Chapters 3, 4 and 5 reduce the centralising force of big money and big government. At present that force compels almost all of us to get and spend national or international money to buy most of the necessities of life and to pay our taxes to our national governments – with the result that, until those national reforms are carried through, the scope for enlarging the role of the local economy and local currencies will inevitably be limited. Once that stifling force is removed,

---

5. See, Colin Hines, *Localization: A Global Manifesto*, Earthscan, 2000, and a perceptive review at http://tinyurl.com/77tushm.

local people will be able to direct their energies more freely to promote local people-centred, green development, and with more enthusiastic support from their local government agencies than is possible under existing conditions.

In short, the dominating power of big money must be reduced in order to liberate the essential role of local economies and local money in people-centred, conserving development. That is one reason why I have concentrated in this book more on the national and international aspects of money system reform than on the future details of local economies and local money.

A final word on that point. In recent years it has been comparatively easy to take part in developing local money systems in support of local economic and social activities of a comparatively marginal kind. It has been much more difficult to lobby effectively for reforms in the national and international money system that will allow local people more freedom to decide how to meet their basic needs in their own localities. So, for the sake of that local freedom, as well as for other reasons, we must give high priority to promoting the national and international aspects of money system reform.

Better co-ordinated local development: the role of money

This section lists a number of points connected with the need for co-ordination between financial, economic, social, ecological and cultural aspects of more self-reliant future local economies.[6]

- Local governments should aim to help local people to become more self-reliant and more conserving.
- Local governments should have a coherent system of local taxation, expenditure, and finance, clearly understandable to local people. They should also support new local socio-economic enterprises such as community currencies, credit unions, community development banks[7] and co-operatives[8].

---

6. Largely taken from my previous books *The Sane Alternative* (1978, 1983), *Future Work* (1985), and *Future Wealth* (1989) – see www.jamesrobertson.com/books.htm. They are still very relevant, especially to the current 'Big Society' idea. 7. Pat Conaty's record, ranging from inner city social enterprises like credit unions and other local Community Development Finance Institutions (CDFI) to Community Land Trusts (see http://tinyurl.com/7284w6h) provides examples of practical actions being taken forward on those lines. 8. 'The UK economy is turning back to the co-operative model to sustain its future'. www.uk.coop/economy2011. Ed Mayo is Secretary General of Co-operatives UK.

- The national government should distribute functions between national and local government in a way that enables average local governments to raise most of the revenue they need to cover their expenditure. The national government should continue to redistribute some income from richer to poorer localities, but in general local governments should depend as little as possible on money from their national (and international) governments.
- The national government should shelter local economies from the full rigour of national and international competition, and allow them to use the purchasing power of local people to foster the local economy by meeting local needs by local work and the use of local resources.
- Local governments should consider contracting out some local public services to local community enterprises. The way 'community contracting' meets the needs of providers as well as users of services can sometimes make it a better alternative to routine delivery by public sector employees than conventional privatisation (commercialisation).
- Local governments should encourage community initiatives in recycling, conservation, allotments, urban farms, horticulture and energy saving, as contributions to more resourceful and conserving communities. They should also encourage local citizens who set up community architecture projects, housing associations, health initiatives, information centres, libraries and other educational and leisure initiatives – both for their own contributions and as potential growth points for other related community initiatives.

All these initiatives should be seen as social investments in the local socio-economy, to be encouraged by national and local government support in the following ways:

- developing techniques of social accounting and social audit, instead of conventionally limited financial accounting and audit, to assess the benefits and costs of community businesses and other community initiatives;
- shifting the emphasis in public sector social spending from dependency-creating services to programmes enabling local communities to meet more of their own needs;
- developing financial and administrative back-up in central and local government, adapted to their increasingly important role as enablers of community enterprises and initiatives;

- encouraging a larger role in local regeneration for trade unions and the voluntary sector, including churches and charities;
- providing management education, adapted to the role of social entrepreneurs committed not to making money for themselves but to creating social well-being.

The question of local unemployment obviously arises.

The top-down approach to the national problem of unemployment is unlikely ever to be successful. Its central weakness is the assumption that useful occupation for unemployed people can only be provided by people who are employed and better off than they are. The assumption that we must depend for work on richer people to provide us with jobs is analogous to the assumption that to make our economy work we must depend on commercial bankers to provide the money supply at a profit to themselves – and is as out-of-date.

The problem of unemployment will probably only be resolved when that top-down approach is seen as complementary – and subordinate – to the aim of encouraging increasing numbers of self-motivated people to undertake worthwhile paid or unpaid work for themselves. Achieving that aim will be one result of the liberating effect of the reforms proposed in Chapters 3 and 4.

Meanwhile, the transition to a society based on ownwork rather than conventional employment will include more self-employment, job-sharing, part-time work, work in small businesses, local co-operatives, community enterprises, and so on. Local governments should be persuaded to remove whatever obstacles they now impose on those and give them what encouragement they can.

Let me end this with the following thought. People-centred development at the local and household levels will reduce the growing burden of ecological, social and economic costs now imposed on us by big business, big money and big government at national and international levels. This applies to people in every country in the world, whether 'developed', 'emerging' or 'poor'.

The people of the world really are all in this together – most of us, anyway. We will need to adjust our minds to greater freedom to control the nature of our work, our family life, our leisure and the balance between them – and to the greater social responsibility that will come with it. If we do that, most of us will almost certainly be able to provide ourselves and our families and neighbours with better opportunities for a good quality of life than if we don't.

CHAPTER 7

Some abstractions and distractions

Many further questions can be raised in discussions about the future of the world's money system. This chapter deals with a few.

I hope what I say will not seem too negative or critical of people from whom I have learned much, and whose intelligence, commitment and goodwill I greatly respect. My comments are based on the need, as I see it, to make and keep the money system as simple and understandable as we possibly can – much more so than it is at present. Otherwise, people and businesses tempted by what the financial experts call 'moral hazard' will continue to use convenient features of it to cheat other people.[1]

Capitalism and Socialism

What should we do to reform the way the money system now works? That is the question this book is about. To that practical question neither 'capitalism' nor 'socialism' now provides us with answers. So far as action is concerned neither of these words has any clear meaning now.

If you take the view that capitalism is the exploitation of man by man and socialism is the precise reverse of that, it is not surprising in this day and age that neither of these obsolescent ideologies can win our confident support. They are tilting at windmills in a battle between tweedledums and tweedledees that distracts valuable energies and resources from purposes that really need them.

I suspect that people who still feel they are supporters of socialism will think this book inclines toward capitalism, and people who still feel they are

---

1. For the meaning of moral hazard see Chapter 4, foonote 4 on page 125.

supporters of capitalism will think the book inclines toward socialism. But in practice it inclines to neither. It simply proposes that:

(a) democratic government agencies serving the public interest should discharge much more effectively than they do today their responsibilities for the rules and scoring system that govern the financial activities of society;
(b) within that framework, independent people and enterprises should be able to work more freely than they can today, both in freer and fairer markets and in ownwork outside the market economy, to provide everyone with needed goods and services.

That does not, of course, mean we can ignore practical present facts that survive from the old ideologies. The following is an example from the UK. Studies show that the Conservative Party is still relying largely on the financial services industry for donations to its funding, "at a time when the Conservative-led government is attempting to kick banking reform into the long grass"; and that the Labour Party still receives over 90% of its funding from the trade unions.[2]

Those are important facts because they help to bias the supposedly democratic process in favour of large and powerful organisations that don't necessarily represent the best interests of the majority of citizens.

There is a short note on lobbying and corruption at the end of this chapter.

Economic growth (and full employment)

The question of economic growth arose in Chapter 2. It was: How can the volume of worldwide economic activity, measured by the total value of money circulating through the economy, grow ad infinitum? Why should it grow ad infinitum? Who – apart from bankers – will have better lives if higher and higher exchanges of money develop ad infinitum between people, businesses and governments?

Economic growth is, frankly, a misconceived national goal. It is closely connected with the equally misconceived goal of full employment, meaning that as many people as possible must be encouraged, and if necessary compelled, to work not for their own purposes but for the purposes of enterprises or people richer and more powerful than themselves. These linked goals of

2. http://tinyurl.com/6556z96 and http://tinyurl.com/7u9b9es.

economic growth and full employment are the outcome of a history that has subordinated the interests of the poor to those of the rich, as described in Chapter 1. They now act as a way of keeping all but the rich and powerful in their place. One of their present results has been identified as the emergence of 'feral' communities at both ends of the social spectrum.[3]

I have written about economic growth previously. For example,

> "Voltaire would surely have ridiculed our concern for Gross National Product, a man-made idol of which we have been persuaded that its size – which only economists know how to measure – is directly proportionate to the happiness of the people of the country over which it presides; an idol, therefore, which has to be fed – in ways which only economists know how to specify – in order to make it as gross as possible." (From my Voltaire Lecture on 'Work: The Right To Be Responsible', 1980 – see Chapter 4, pp. 60-61, of *Beyond The Dependency Culture.*[4])

As well as Tim Jackson (see Chapter 2, footnote 3), the 'post-autistic economics' movement[5] and latterly the 'degrowth' movement[6] have become prominent in a growing academic reaction against economic growth as the goal of economic policy. These could potentially unfreeze conventional academic opinion in the course of time. But we need practical change much sooner.

Gold and other commodities

In financially difficult times such as these, cries go up in favour of 'real money' based on the value of something valuable like gold, instead of today's 'fiat money' which is created out of thin air and authorised to serve the public interest.

Return to gold?

Keynes' view that the gold standard was a 'barbarous relic' has always seemed right to me. We humans ought now to be intelligent enough not to allow ourselves to be bound to the value of a traditionally magic metal, the value of which fluctuates according to how much of it exists, who owns

3. http://tinyurl.com/3z6kakx. 4. www.jamesrobertson.com/books.htm#dependency.
5. www.paecon.net/HistoryPAE.htm. 6. www.degrowth.org.

how much of it, and what price it happens to be fetching in the market. The built-in effect of going back to the gold standard would be to bias money values in favour of people, businesses and nations powerful or fortunate enough to capture the ownership of more gold than others – as in pre-democratic times.

I continue to take that view. The fact that buying gold over the past few years has been very good for people who are now sitting on sizeable profits for themselves, does not mean that the value of gold should recover its historical role as the basis for the world's money system. They could also be sitting on other temporarily successful investments – prestigious works of art, for instance – but we wouldn't think of basing our currency on those.

Powerful arguments in favour of a return to the gold standard are, however, now being put forward. I recommend the following to readers who would welcome examples: Keith Hudson, in the following and earlier posts on http://tinyurl.com/6rmb7jg; and James Turk http://tinyurl.com/83vy4vu. They argue that the creation of fiat money out of thin air has inevitably led to the creation of too much.

But it is equally possible to argue that the reason why that has happened is that:

(1) it is the commercial banks who have been allowed to create the money supply as profit-making business;
(2) central banks working in the public interest as agencies of society have not had the power to control it in the public interest by creating it themselves debt-free; and
(3) monetary reform, giving central banks the responsibility of creating the money supply themselves, will make it easier to control the amount of money created.

Other commodities

Similar arguments can be brought against proposals to base currencies on the value of 'baskets of commodities'. These baskets could include selections from long lists of resources like oil, grain, cotton, gold, coffee, carbon emissions and so on.

A huge amount of sophisticated work has been done on these proposals. But I have a confession to make. I find it too difficult to understand how they would work and how they would be managed *as currencies*[7] and I suspect it will be too difficult for most other people to understand that either. So, if the attempt to base a national or world currency on any such basket were ever introduced, I can't see how it could succeed. Although Nathan Lewis, the author of the following remarks, was defending the gold standard, I had some sympathy with it when I read it.

> "From time to time, some smarty-pants proposes that it makes sense to peg a currency to a commodity basket, rather than to gold. The basic idea is the same, but they think that a commodity basket is a better representation of stable monetary value than gold is. Typically, Mr. Smarty Pants thinks this is a new insight, and that he should win the Nobel Prize for his contribution to humanity. Like most ideas in economics, it is a very old idea."[8]

Rationing and trading

As mentioned in the Introduction, the growing range of profit-based schemes for rationing harmful environmental activities like the emission of carbon into the atmosphere has not been effective. Some have actually given sizeable windfall profits to heavily polluting companies; others have been outright scams.

Chapter 5 noted that at the international level these schemes had assumed that climate change is the overriding ecological threat we face, and that the environment's capacity to absorb carbon emissions is the only environmental resource to which we need apply the principle of contraction and convergence.[9] But, as it also pointed out, dealing with questions like these piecemeal without full regard to interactions between them, can lead to serious mistakes. For example, to encourage the growth of biofuels to replace carbon-emitting fuels can have disastrous results.[10] One is the destruction of forests

---

7. I see how they can provide the basis for private contracts, investments or insurance policies, but not how they can provide a basis for public currencies. 8. 'Gold is Stable in Value 4: More Commodities Prices, and Commodity Baskets', see http://tinyurl.com/74l4sft. 9. This principle goes back quite a long time. I don't claim to have invented it myself, but in 1983 I was writing in *The Sane Alternative*, page 41, that "the SHE (sane, humane, ecological) path of development will lead the peoples of the world's rich and poor countries to converge around an adequate and sustainable level of material consumption" — in contrast to the HE scenario that the richest countries would continue to lead the rest along a 'hyperexpansionist' path. 10. See, for example, http://tinyurl.com/7x65tja.

to clear the land to grow biofuels, which forgets that forests meet a range of other ecological needs – some related directly to climate change, and others for different purposes like the preservation of biodiversity. Another shameful result is the conversion of agricultural land needed to grow essential food for people in poor countries into land growing crops to produce biofuels for people in rich countries.

The practical question now is how to implement the principle of contraction and convergence. Should it be by different schemes for rationing different environmental resources like the world's capacity to absorb carbon emissions and for encouraging businesses and people to trade their surplus rations? Or should it be by a much more general reconstruction of taxation and public spending, as I recommend?

Let us look at the problems with the global and national schemes designed to ration carbon emissions and encourage recipients to sell their surplus rations.

Broadly speaking, the global scheme based on the one originally developed by Aubrey Meyer[11] and actually called 'Contraction and Convergence' requires international agreement on:

(1) the overall limit to the sustainable quantity of CO_2 in the atmosphere;
(2) the date by which current global emissions should fall to that target;
(3) the year-by-year allocation of permits to countries to emit CO_2 to achieve that global target; and
(4) the principle that all countries should eventually be entitled to an equal per capita level of CO_2 emissions.

Countries needing more than their allocated limit are able to buy permits from countries not needing to use all theirs.

The late David Fleming[12] developed a comparable national scheme to reduce CO_2 emissions and distribute oil, gas and electric power fairly to people:

(1) every adult would be given tradable energy quotas (TEQs) of an equal number of units, whereas industry and government would have to bid to buy units at a weekly tender;
(2) to start with, a full year's supply of units would be issued and then, every week as units were used, the number in circulation would be topped up with a further week's supply;

11. http://tinyurl.com/6ua3b5b. 12. http://tinyurl.com/24vcaeu.

(3) units could be traded between those who needed less and those who needed more than the allocation;
(4) when you bought energy, e.g. electricity for your household, units would be deducted automatically from your TEQ;
(5) the total number of units in circulation would be decided by an independent Energy Policy Committee in a TEQs Budget, looking 20 years ahead, and the number would go down week-by-week, step-by-step; and
(6) the government would itself be bound by the scheme; it would learn to live within it, and how to help the rest of us to do so too.

Those schemes have been the outcome of dedicated, skilled work. On paper they are logical, clear and impressive. But, as mentioned previously, implementing the 1997 Kyoto Protocol has been a hard grind. The European Union Greenhouse Gas Emissions Trading Scheme, which only began operating in January 2005, is already under fire for giving big quotas to corporations with huge carbon emissions, who can easily meet them and have surplus quotas to sell. So instead of 'polluter pays', we get 'polluters will be paid'.

Serious practical problems face all rationing and trading schemes:

(1) The target for the total sustainable use of a particular resource, and the date for achieving it, will be disputed.
(2) So will the question of who should be in the scheme.
(3) So will decisions about who gets what rations: should more important people (like leaders in government and business, and workers in public services) get higher rations than other people? — a huge potential source of dispute, corruption and mistrust.
(4) What enforcing system will ensure that rations are not exceeded and that trading them is free from fraud?
(5) Will letting the rich buy surpluses be accepted as fair?
(6) How many similar rationing schemes will eventually proliferate for other scarce environmental resources?
(7) Will a growing number of different markets in trading rights to use a growing number of different resources turn the money system into an even bigger mess than it is already?

There is, I am sure, a preferable alternative. The principle of contraction and convergence can be implemented more widely, effectively and understandably by changing what is now taxed and what public spending is now spent on at national level (as proposed in Chapter 4), and by the new developments in global taxing and spending (as proposed in Chapter 5).

A note on corruption

As the The Global Infrastructure Anti-Corruption Centre (GIACC) has written:

> "There is no international legal definition of corruption. In its narrowest sense, corruption is interpreted as referring to bribery and extortion. In its wider sense, corruption includes one or more of bribery, extortion, fraud, deception, collusion, cartels, abuse of power, embezzlement, trading in influence and money laundering. These activities will normally constitute criminal offences in most jurisdictions although the precise definition of the offence may differ."[13]

Corruption is a very wide and varied concept. At one extreme, critics could go so far as to suggest that the money system itself is a basically corrupt system. At the other, it can be argued that each activity should be examined on its merits in order to establish whether or not it should be regarded as corrupt. Somewhere in the middle, it will be possible to discover what aspects of dealing with money are treated as criminal and which are not.

Corruption is a huge subject in its own right and we do not have the space to go into it more deeply, but the notes include some references for anyone who wants to explore the subject further.[14]

---

13. The Global Infrastructure Anti-Corruption Centre (GIACC), http://tinyurl.com/7zetcq2.
14. (1) Political Cleanup, http://political-cleanup.org. (2) Transparency International UK, www.transparency.org.uk. (3) Unlock Democracy, http://tinyurl.com/879ntfh.

CONCLUSION

So what's to be done? And how?

In recent months, public reaction against the way the money system now works has continued to spread. In the two countries I know best, Britain and the United States, positive public campaigns have been building up, backed by well-documented proposals for reform and increasing contact with national legislatures.[1]

I hope this book will help to spread understanding of what needs to be done, and how it can be done.

The money system of today has developed from the Anglo-American empires of the past two centuries into a single worldwide system. As it now works, it causes systemic inefficiency, ecological destruction and injustice in almost every sphere of life. It is as if Satan had imposed a perverse calculus of values on us,[2] which compels or encourages almost everyone in the world to compete against one another for a greater share of planetary resources and, in doing so, to turn them into waste. It is now urgent that we redevelop the money system and start managing it purposefully to reconcile money values with ecological and social values.

That is the only way to resolve the problems the financial 'experts' now find insoluble. When will they notice the unsound foundation on which the money system now rests? When will they see that the present foundation is an obsolete leftover from how governments carried out their functions in a pre-democratic age, before the need to live within the limits of the planet's resources was recognised?

Organised practical action to change the way the money system works is

---

1. Two examples are the American Monetary Institute (Stephen Zarlenga), www.monetary.org, and the Positive Money Campaign (Ben Dyson), www.positivemoney.org.uk. 2. See 'Devil's Tunes', Chapter 10 in *Beyond the Dependency Culture*, www.jamesrobertson.com/books.htm#dependency.

now vital for our well-being and survival. It is unrealistic to suppose that other well-meaning advice will do the trick – such as 'We must all learn to love one another', or 'We must replace money with a gift economy', or 'We just have to change our minds', or 'We must be the change ourselves', or 'All we have to do is to stop sinning' or 'Abolish capitalism', and so forth.

It is more helpful to see the money system working as it does now because it is diseased; and to understand how its disease could be fatal for us as a species, just as a diseased blood system or nervous system may be fatal to a living person. That would call for a diagnosis and a cure that gets to the root of the disease. It would then require us to make sure that the cure is carried out.

This book has shown that the disease has been caused by the unspoken purposes of a money system inherited from the past. It has proposed the cure set out in Chapters 3 to 6. The question now is: how can we make sure that the cure is put into practice?

Strong worldwide opposition to money system reform may well continue from the still-growing body of more or less reputable professionals and their families, friends and associates around the world who benefit from the status quo. They make an unusually comfortable living from the money system, the tentacles of which exert power and influence in many walks of life – politicians, bankers, government officials, investment managers, accountants, tax consultants, financial advisers, insurance experts, economists and countless others.

Naturally enough, few of those people will be eager to admit that the money system may be in need of radical reform – from its roots up. Many of the younger people among them may be concerned for their future career prospects. Older people, who have been responsible for managing parts of the money system as it has been working, may see the prospect of its radical reform not only as a personal financial threat but also as an attack on their self-esteem, implying that they have spent their working lives in ways that may have been worthless or worse. We will have to understand and even sympathise with how they feel, without allowing them to sabotage the changes that need to be made.[3]

3. Joseph Huber, reminding me recently about Thomas Kuhn's theory of scientific paradigm shift in *The Structure of Scientific Revolutions*, 1962, said: "People do not normally give up their convictions, even if these have become untenable, because this would be too threatening to what they see as their identity and their professional and economic existence. They combat against the challenge or challengers – as long as they manage to defend their status; or, as time goes by, until they become marginalised and die out. That's what Kuhn called the 'biological solution' to competing paradigms and to the struggle between conservative and progressive positions". Unfortunately however, in this case we may not have enough time to wait for the 'biological solution'.

That means we have to recognise that, for the time being, probably only a minority – but a growing minority – of active money-system practitioners and professionals will want to support the proposed reforms. They will mainly be from among the most able younger men and women. They won't necessarily be inspired only by ethical considerations. Clear-sighted career ambition could also attract them to participate early in the new departure in the history of money they see coming.

Turning to other sections of society, we must take a lead from Machiavelli. As he pointed out in 1532 in *The Prince,* "he who introduces a new order of things has all those who profit from the old order as enemies, and he has only lukewarm allies in all those who might profit from the new."

That is very true – it seems fairly obvious once you think about it. We need to take it seriously and recognise its consequences.

For example, a multitude of charities, pressure groups and non-governmental organisations (NGOs) – and governmental agencies too, for that matter – are concerned with good causes of every kind everywhere in the world. These include environmental issues (climate change, energy supply and use, water, food and agriculture etc.); social issues (poverty, welfare, social injustice, health, human rights etc); general public policy and economic issues (world future prospects; local and community economic development; ethical investing, trading and consuming; corporate social responsibility); and the challenges faced by religious and spiritual faiths in engaging with the world today.

So why do we hear so few of these bodies protesting against governments for allowing commercial banks to create the money supply as profit-making debt, or allowing the rich to pay lower taxes than the poor in proportion to their incomes and wealth?

It could be because they are all preoccupied with raising money from the money system as it now works in order to support their activities. So they feel they cannot afford the time and money or the risk involved in campaigning for changes in it – even though it is a principal cause of the ills they are supposed to be dealing with.

We must realise that we are all motivated by how we personally perceive the balance of risk and reward we face between different courses of action open to us at any particular time. Where money-system reform is concerned, that applies not only to people directly concerned with money, and to the press and broadcasting media, but to many other people too. To some extent, the careers, reputations, earnings, pensions and investments of thousands of influential people in our legislatures and press and broadcasting industries as well as banking, finance and government are directly affected by the fortunes of the banking industry.

So we have to ask ourselves how it will be possible, in the face of active opposition and understandable inertia, to put the necessary reforms of the world's money system into practice quickly enough to save the future of our civilisation. The challenge can be seen as comparable to the one Antonio Gramsci described in his letters and notebooks from prison in 1929. It calls for "pessimism of the intellect" (we must recognise that the obstacles to necessary changes appear overwhelming) and "optimism of the will" (we must nevertheless do what we can to make the changes happen).

Although we remain confident of somehow breaking through to a new more civilised money system to serve the interests of the people of the world, it is not easy to predict precisely when and where the tipping point or tipping points will come that will trigger self-reinforcing progress toward success.

This is where the most important actors of all come in – namely us. As active citizens all over the world, we must press our governments, NGOs, businesses and educational enterprises to give high priority to money-system reform. In that context, two sets of people may have special parts to play.

First, although women are now making conspicuous contributions to new thinking on the future of money, the way the money system actually works is still based on the values of overgrown boys competing to make higher scores in games they play with our money. Although women have been prominent participants in the recent 'Arab Spring', in Western countries they are now, in general, being treated worse than men by government policies aimed at clearing up the mess after the men's games.

Second, in many countries *young people* today are being notably badly treated by the way the money system is working. Many are now protesting and demonstrating powerfully against it, as they are in various parts of the world against other features of unjust societies too. They must be supported in putting their energies constructively behind the radical changes needed in how the money system works.

There is one last point to mention. Growing communication between groups of citizens in different countries who share common campaigning aims on particular aspects of money system reform – such as how the money supply is created and managed or the need for shifts in taxes and public spending (Chapters 3 and 4) – can help to increase the support given to those proposals in their own countries. By contrast, opponents of such proposals will pressurise their governments to co-ordinate their policies on these matters with other governments in order to hold them back to the speed of the slowest ship in the convoy. Given the urgency of these reforms, any government convinced of the need for them may have to implement them independently without waiting for the laggards to catch up.

Over thirty years ago, in *The Sane Alternative,* I suggested that "more and more people believe that the human race must break through to a new kind of future. Failure will mean disaster; success will mean an important upward step on the ladder of evolutionary progress. Many of us see this breakthrough as the central project, the historic task, for the two or three generations living at the present time — the task which gives meaning to our lives."[4]

Since then we haven't made very much progress – the reverse, in many ways. But the 21st-century world community has come closer together; worldwide mass communication, including person-to-person contact through the internet, has become a reality; we share growing awareness of living on the same planet as one another; and in almost every country increasing numbers of us are aspiring to play our part in society in conditions of economic and social justice.

I have suggested in this book a response to the present global financial collapse which gets to the root of its cause. It can help us to prolong the life of our species and to 'break through to a new kind of future'. We now need to mobilise the collective statesmanship to put it into practice.

---

4. www.jamesrobertson.com/books.htm#sane, page 1.

APPENDIX 1

The Georgist and Social Credit movements

This Appendix briefly expands the reference to the Georgist and Social Credit Movements in the section on the 'stand-off between economics and ethics' in Chapter 2.

Georgism grew up towards the end of the 19th century and continues to flourish as an international movement. Among its prominent centres today are the International Union for Land Value Taxation and its website links,[1] and the Henry George Foundation and its links.[2]

Henry George (1839-1897) was not an academic economist; he reached his conclusions from real-life experience; and he attracted a worldwide 'Georgist' movement in support of them.

After ending his formal education at fourteen and working his way up in the newspaper business, Henry George wrote his ground-breaking book, *Progress and Poverty* (1879),[3] in response to his experience in California of the dramatic rise in land values caused by the arrival of the railways. He proposed that all other taxes be replaced by a tax on the annual value of land held as private property. That tax would reduce the unearned profit to landowners from rising land values, create a fairer balance between landowners and the people whose work helped to make land values rise, and motivate landowners to use the land well. Broadening George's proposed tax shift to include taxes on the value of other environmental resources and combining it with a Citizen's Income, as proposed in Chapter 4, will be big steps toward J.S. Mill's aim of "uniting the greatest individual liberty of action with a

---

1. www.theiu.org. 2. www.henrygeorgefoundation.org. 3. http://progressandpoverty.org.

common ownership in the raw material of the globe".

Georgism is relevant to us today not just for the positive merits of the tax shift it proposes. It is also notable for the hostility of the economists who, funded by US banks and financial institutions and big business land-holders like the railroad companies, campaigned to have its ideas excluded from the academic economics agenda.[4]

At the national level in Britain, Henry George's ideas made better political progress. The Liberal government's People's Budget of 1909 proposed the introduction of a land tax based on Henry George's thinking. But, having been hotly opposed by the aristocratic landlords in the House of Lords, the Liberals dropped it in the course of the subsequent political and parliamentary shake-up; the outbreak of the Great War in 1914 then distracted attention from the land tax issue; after the war, the socialism of Labour replaced the Liberal agenda with a basically different agenda; and, from 1945 until the 1990s, the attention of Western democracies was focused on the conflict with communism. Only in the last few years has land value tax begun to revive as an item for serious political discussion.

This UK experience has a lesson for us today: good progress towards a critically important reform is not enough; until it is finally implemented as a long-term fixture, it can suffer a bad setback and be kept off the mainstream political agenda for a hundred years.

C. H. Douglas (1879-1952), the founder of the Social Credit movement,[5] was also not an academic economist; he was a Scottish engineer. His working experience with manufacturing companies in the early years of the 20th century brought him up against problems arising from how money was created and put into circulation as debt by banks in the form of profit-making loans to their customers. His detailed analysis of these problems is not very easy to follow. But it led him to suggest measures combining a proposal for a monetary reform – making money creation a public service – with a proposal to distribute a National Dividend – comparable to what we now call a basic income or Citizen's Income.

This book's Chapters 3 and 4 propose monetary reform and a Citizen's Income, along with taxing the values of land and other common resources

4. Those campaigns are well documented by Mason Gaffney and Fred Harrison in *The Corruption of Economics*, Shepheard-Walwyn. http://tinyurl.com/7746vot.
5. http://en.wikipedia.org/wiki/Social_Credit.

that are diverted to private profit, as key features of a money system modernised for the 21st century.

Two further points on the Georgist and Social Credit movements are worth mentioning.

First, some supporters of one or the other have seemed to suggest that, compared with the crucial importance of the reform they support themselves, the proposals of the other will make little useful contribution to a better world. It is good to know that leading supporters of each have now got beyond that self-centred stage and recognise that campaigners for land value taxation and monetary reform can help each other to achieve their aims.[6]

In general, it is important to avoid such a NIH (Not Invented Here) syndrome. It is a trap that otherwise well-meaning people can fall into when, having worked out their own solutions to problems, they mistakenly oppose other people's proposals that may be complementary to theirs. A similar case is the misguided opposition between some narrowly focused advocates of local, national or international monetary reform, who assume that whichever of those monopolises their own attention is the only important one. "Only connect". Making your potential allies into opponents gives joy to the hearts of enemies of the causes that you both support.

Second, the development of the Georgist and Social Credit movements should continue to fascinate serious students of economic and social history. But I wouldn't insist that people who want to help to change the money system today should spend too much time and energy getting bogged down trying to master the details of those two movements. In past years I was put off both of them for some time by the embattled one-track minds of some of their then protagonists – and by the unusual historical meanings the Georgists gave to terms like 'rent', and the complexities of the new institutional arrangements the Social Crediters proposed. It was only later in retrospect that I realised the proposals of the Georgists and Social Crediters resembled my practical conclusions about the need for monetary reform, taxation of the value subtracted from common resources, and a Citizen's Income.

---

6. A good example is Alanna Hartzok, Earthrights Institute, www.earthrights.net.

APPENDIX 2

Contacts for further study and research, selected references and acknowledgements*

This Appendix brings together some of the people and organisations actively engaged with the future of money, many of whom have already been mentioned in various chapters. Its purpose is to provide a collection of starting points that readers may find useful if they want to go more deeply into topics discussed in the book.

The list is by no means complete. There are many other people from whom I have learned over the years, and to whom I am grateful.

Following a General section, the entries are shown in sections broadly corresponding to the topics discussed in different chapters of the book.

General (includes various aspects of the money system and related topics)

new economics foundation: www.neweconomics.org/. Director **Stewart Wallis.** Wide-ranging contributions to topics this book discusses. Trustee **James Skinner** is a supporter of monetary reform.

Forum for the Future: www.forumforthefuture.org. Not specifically about money or economics, but many references to them are at http://tinyurl.com/7vk4jtu. Also see **Jonathon Porritt**'s articles at http://tinyurl.com/ch2uuhs.

Hazel Henderson: www.hazelhenderson.com/recent_papers.html: essential, widespread coverage of the future of the money system from a US viewpoint. Also find her under 'Ethical Uses of Money' below.

David Korten: http://livingeconomiesforum.org Another broad and essential US contribution. Closely associated with **YES!** *magazine***,** www.yesmagazine.org.

---

* This Appendix together with all the footnotes in this book can be found as live links at www.greenbooks.co.uk/Future-Money.html and at www.jamesrobertson.com/future-money.htm.

The late Richard Douthwaite (Ireland): Takes a wide view of money. His books include *The Ecology of Money*. For details of them and himself, see Green Books' website http://tinyurl.com/7yv7nng. He was a founder of **Feasta** (The Foundation for the Economics of Sustainability, www.feasta.org).

Margrit Kennedy: http://tinyurl.com/792sn52 (Germany). Comprehensive approach to Money – see http://tinyurl.com/7mda8c4.

Bernard Lietaer: Also a comprehensive approach. 'Currency Solutions for a Wiser World', http://tinyurl.com/82cuca2.

James Bruges and **Marion Wells:** Active Quakers supportive to progressive projects in India and the UK. James Bruges' books are *The Little Earth Book*, the *Big Earth Book*, and *The Biochar Debate* – see http://tinyurl.com/7axjl7c.

Steven B. Kurtz: A philosopher member of the Canadian Association for the Club of Rome, circulates information and ideas on a wide range of topics broadly related to those at http://tinyurl.com/859s6os.

Shann Turnbull: Australian Principal of the International Institute for Self-governance, concerned with wide-ranging financial innovations. http://tinyurl.com/709exmx.

Caroline Lucas, MP: Green Party leader (England and Wales), www.carolinelucas.com/cl.html – promotes many policies in Parliament supporting fairer and greener use of public finances.

Molly Scott Cato: UK Green Party speaker on economic issues, and Director of Cardiff Institute for Co-operative Studies. http://tinyurl.com/6rxf54j. Author of *Green Economics: An Introduction to Theory, Policy and Practice.*

Martin Large: *Common Wealth: For a free, equal, mutual and sustainable society*, Hawthorn Press, 2010. http://tinyurl.com/7bfgo8r. Reviewed at www.jamesrobertson.com/news-jan10.htm, Item 4.1.

Ellen LaConte (USA): *LIFE RULES: Why so much is going wrong everywhere at once and how Life teaches us to fix it*, iUniverse, 2010. http://tinyurl.com/85z6zun. Also Blog at www.ellenlaconte.com/edge-wise.

Keith Hudson: http://allisstatus.wordpress.com. Comments on evolution and human social and economic life – very stimulating; sometimes arguable, for example on restoring the gold standard.

Diana Schumacher: Wide-ranging contributor to new economics. http://tinyurl.com/708ukyz.

George Monbiot: http://tinyurl.com/87ehkvb. "From now on, as the old dream dies, nothing is straightforward. But at least we have the beginning of a plan". Many of his articles listed along with 'Out of the Ashes' raise important questions about money. (I question his support for nuclear power, mainly because its exceptional risks for security and health enable policy-makers and managers to justify a damaging lack of transparency and accountability.)

Bruce Nixon: His excellent new book, *A better world is possible – what needs to be done and how we can make it happen,* is at www.brucenixon.com/betterworld.html. I wish him well with it.

Charles Bazlinton: Blogspot www.the-free-lunch.blogspot.com regularly comments on UK monetary reform, land value taxation and Citizen's Income. 'Fairness with freedom' should attract us all.

New Era Network: http://neweranetwork.info. Main concerns: promoting the health of people and the planet, localising economic activity now too centralised, and peacefully reconciling conflict. See the list of networkers. It is also connected with the Attwood Group – details at http://thomasattwood.wordpress.com.

Samuel Brittan and **Martin Wolf:** Two highly respected *Financial Times* commentators.

Samuel Brittan has recently written in favour of land value taxation: http://www.samuelbrittan.co.uk/text419_p.html.

So has Martin Wolf: "Land value taxation is a 'no-brainer' . . . It is both fair and efficient. It should be adopted." See http://tinyurl.com/7x9yrxx. He has also criticised how the money supply is now created: "The essence of the contemporary monetary system is creation of money, out of nothing, by private banks' often foolish lending", see http://tinyurl.com/75la49k.

Ann Pettifor: www.debtonation.org. This blog on 'Debt, Credit & the International Financial System' provides a gateway to over 70 subjects ranging from Anglo-American financial crisis to World Bank – by way of Debt, Euro and Euroland, Globalisation, Green New Deal, Keynes, Public Spending, and the UK Financial Crisis. Highly recommended.

Ethical uses of money

Hazel Henderson: *Ethical Markets: Growing the Green Economy* (2007), see www.ethicalmarkets.com.

Laszlo Solnai: Director, Business Ethics Center, Corvinus University, Budapest, see http://laszlo-zsolnai.net.

Tarek El Diwany: He explains Islamic teaching – *The Problem With Interest,* Kreatoc Ltd, 3rd edition, 2010. http://tinyurl.com/7lm9mbg.

Canon Peter Challen: The Christian Council for Monetary Justice, www.ccmj.org.

St Paul's Institute: (Its former Director, Canon Giles Fraser, resigned from the Cathedral in late October, 2011 in response to how it proposed to deal with the 'anti-capitalist' demonstrators outside its doors.) www.stpaulsinstitute.org.uk.

Fr. Sean Healy and **Sr. Brigid Reynolds** are now leading Social Justice Ireland: see www.socialjustice.ie/content/about-us. A **Basic Income** has been an important feature of their work for more than a quarter of a century with CORI Justice.

Ecumenical Council for Corporate Responsibility: http://tinyurl.com/88vsujo.

Ekklesia: Beliefs and values thinktank on religion, politics, theology, culture and society – www.ekklesia.co.uk.

How the money supply should be created and managed

Ben Dyson: Positive Money (www.positivemoney.org.uk), the leading UK campaign for monetary reform, making really good progress.

Stephen Zarlenga: Director of the American Monetary Institute which is actively campaigning for monetary reform in USA and making really good progress too. Also ground-breaking book *The Lost Science of Money: The Mythology of Money – The Story of Power*: see www.monetary.org.

Prosperity (**Alistair McConnachie**): http://prosperityuk.com, leading pioneer of monetary reform – see the important list of links to relevant people and organisations.

new economics foundation
(1) with **Ben Dyson** and **Prof. Richard Werner**, submission to UK Independent Commission on Banking, January 2011 at http://tinyurl.com/85empgz, and
(2) with **Prof. Richard Werner** and **Andrew Jackson**, 'Where does money come from? A guide to the UK monetary and banking system', September 2011. http://tinyurl.com/4yk5zqt.

Joseph Huber and **James Robertson:** *Creating New Money: A Monetary Reform for the Information Age*, New Economics Foundation, 2000, www.jamesrobertson.com/books.htm#creating.

Joseph Huber: *Monetative*: *Taking Money Creation back into Public Hands.* (Germany). http://tinyurl.com/75hxqba.

Mary Mellor: *The Future of Money: From Financial Crisis to Public Resource*, 2010. Essential reading on the money system and its future from an 'anti-capitalist' viewpoint. See my review at Item 2.(1) at www.jamesrobertson.com/news-jul10.htm#bookreviews.

Bill Still (USA): supporting monetary reform, *The Moneymasters* and *The Secret of Oz*. Highly recommended films and text. See www.themoneymasters.com/mm.

Ellen Hodgson Brown (USA): *The Web of Debt: The Shocking Truth About Our Money System And How We Can Break Free, 2009*, acclaimed as "an absolute must read and relevant to people of all political stripes" – book and follow-up blog at www.webofdebt.com.

Simon Dixon: After experience in the City of London, he campaigns for a fundamental monetary reform, advises on the financial crisis, and prepares the next generation of UK banking leaders for the future. See www.simondixon.org.

Ann Belsey at the **Money Reform Party**: Informative, interesting website – see http://tinyurl.com/89bm4j3.

Frances Hutchinson: *Understanding The Financial System: Social Credit Rediscovered,* Jon Carpenter Publishing, 2010, see my review at www.jamesrobertson.com/news-jan11.htm, Item 3.(3).

John Lanchester: *Whoops! Why everyone owes everyone and no one can pay,* Penguin, 2010, http://tinyurl.com/7almbt8. "A devastating and devastatingly funny analysis of the credit crunch and subsequent global financial meltdown", *London Review of Books*. One of the best of many books on the credit crunch.

Shifts in taxes and other sources of public revenue

To capture land value by taxation (with links to the Georgist movement)

Fred Harrison: His blog – www.fredharrison.com – is a 'must read'. His *The Power in the Land* and other books are a prime source for the wide-ranging economic and social arguments for land value tax (LVT). See http://tinyurl.com/7pn4trp.

Alanna Hartzok: www.earthrights.net/about/hartzok.html. Includes projects in USA and Africa, as well as for United Nations. For full coverage see www.earthrightsinstitute.net and www.earthrightsinstitute.org.

The **Coalition for Economic Justice:** A recently established coalition of think tanks, charities and pressure groups supporting the introduction of an annual Land Value Tax (LVT) to replace or reduce existing taxes on enterprise and labour. www.c4ej.com. See its listed member organisations.

'Land&Liberty' – www.LandandLiberty.net – is the quarterly magazine of the Henry George Foundation in London.

Tony Vickers chairs Action for Land Taxation and Economic Reform (ALTER): www.libdemsalter.org.uk – see their excellent 'Quotes' at http://tinyurl.com/7x9yrxx.

Robert Schalkenbach Foundation (USA): http://schalkenbach.org is an exceptional source of information about the proposals of Henry George and their influence today – see, for example, **Prof. Mason Gaffney**'s important contribution on Henry George's relevance today at http://tinyurl.com/7umcool.

The IU – International Union for Land Value Taxation: is a global non-governmental organisation established in 1926 to promote permanent peace and prosperity by re-establishing mankind's natural relationship with land – www.theiu.org.

To capture the value of other environmental resources by taxation

A **UK parliamentary report** concluded in July 2011: "There is a pressing need for Government to take a more coherent and clearly articulated approach to environmental taxes". http://tinyurl.com/7l5yuxc.

Prof. Paul Ekins: www.ucl.ac.uk/cbes/people/paul-ekins (Energy Institute, University College, London):

(1) Green Fiscal Commission www.greenfiscalcommission.org.uk
(2) Theory and Practice of Environmental Taxation
http://tinyurl.com/7oxlw4k.

David Gee: European Environment Agency: http://tinyurl.com/6pxwjtt.

To reduce tax avoidance

John Christensen: 'Tax Havens Cause Poverty'. A 'must read'.
http://tinyurl.com/ykqodjt.

Richard Murphy: http://tinyurl.com/4lej4b. Another powerful call to action.

Prof. Prem Sikka: http://tinyurl.com/7b7qsg3. For too cosy relationships between government and tax avoiders, see http://tinyurl.com/7jpa24v.

Shifts in public spending

Shift – to a Citizen's Income (or Basic Income)

Citizen's Income Trust: www.citizensincome.org (Director, **Malcolm Torry**) reports on the feasibility of a citizen's income in the UK.

Basic Income Earth Network (BIEN): www.basicincome.org/bien. Chair, International Advisory Board, **Philippe Van Parijs.** For Basic Income News, see http://binews.org.

The U.S. Basic Guarantee Network (USBIG), Karl Widerquist: Promotes discussion of the basic income guarantee in the United States. See http://usbig.net.

Shift – away from

(1) Cost of government debt (see Chapter 3)
(2) Perverse subsidies
(3) Contracts to the private sector
(4) Other wasteful public spending (see Chapter 4)

Norman Myers: *Perverse Subsidies: Tax $s Undercutting Our Economies and Environments Alike*. See http://tinyurl.com/827rthz and also http://tinyurl.com/6usbktm.

Guardian Datablog Guide to Private Finance Initiative:
http://tinyurl.com/7hzd3zx. November 2010.

George Monbiot on **Private Finance Initiative:** http://tinyurl.com/6mnnwhh.

Private Finance Initiative for Hospitals: http://tinyurl.com/7hlcj8o. January 2011.

International money

Herbie Girardet, http://tinyurl.com/6rlonfo and **Jakob von Uexkull** http://tinyurl.com/79qacgs founded the **World Future Council:** www.worldfuturecouncil.org. For a financial proposal that would be a step toward a genuinely international new currency for international transactions, see www.worldfuturecouncil.org/new_money.html.

Nicholas Hildyard and **Larry Lohmann, The Corner House:** Why carbon rationing and trading won't work. See 'Carry on Polluting' at http://tinyurl.com/6nbrk9c. (Their finding was later supported by **Lord (Adair) Turner**, see http://tinyurl.com/yjhw8mw).

Wendy Harcourt: Will the Society for International Development (SID) take seriously the need for money system reform to support "systemic change in politics, economic, military, gender hierarchies, and social systems"? In her editorial for Development, January 2012, Wendy Harcourt sees economic justice as central to future development, and people everywhere wanting to hold the financial system accountable for the deep inequalities ripping through societies. See http://tinyurl.com/87x9vzp.

John Bunzl and **SIMPOL:** http://simpol.org.uk. A democratic campaign to get legislators in different countries to support simultaneous introduction of reforms needed to save the planet. Global grassroots co-operation in action. Well worth exploring further.

Local community currencies and financial enterprises

Rob Hopkins: 'Transition Towns', http://tinyurl.com/3us2lqt and www.transitionbooks.net (local currencies shown on right).

David Boyle: www.david-boyle.co.uk.
Tom Greco (USA): www.reinventingmoney.com.
(For comments on these two distinguished thinkers see www.jamesrobertson.com/news-jun09.htm, Item 4(3)&(4) and Item 5.)

The late Richard Douthwaite (Ireland): Also see under 'General' above. http://tinyurl.com/88tq43u.

David Korten and **YES! Magazine** (USA): Also at 'General' above. http://tinyurl.com/7lazqvr.

new economics foundation: See website entries for 'Local Money' – http://tinyurl.com/7b7rn90.

New Economics Institute (USA): http://neweconomicsinstitute.org.

John Rogers: http://localcurrency.wordpress.com.

Colin Hines: *Localization: A Global Manifesto* – http://tinyurl.com/6679az6, Earthscan, 2000. Excellent book. But **David Cromwell**'s perceptive review asked the key question raised by all these localisation proposals: will opposition and public inertia let them happen? http://tinyurl.com/77tushm.

Pat Conaty: Credit Unions, other local Community Development Finance Institutions (CDFI), Community Land Trusts, etc. – see http://tinyurl.com/7284w6h.

Ed Mayo: Secretary General of Co-operatives UK, which reported in 2011 that "the UK economy is turning back to the co-operative model to sustain its future" – see www.uk.coop.

A few concluding references to corruption

Political Cleanup: http://political-cleanup.org.

The Global Infrastructure Anti-Corruption Centre (GIACC): http://tinyurl.com/7zetcq2.

Transparency International UK: www,transparency.org.uk.

Unlock Democracy: http://tinyurl.com/879ntfh.

Finally, I end this list with grateful acknowledgements to:

John Elford for the skill and commitment and patience with which he and **Stacey Hedge** and his other colleagues at Green Books have brought this book to publication.

Francis Miller (www.miller-consulting.co.uk) for his contributions to the book, in the course of helping me to manage my website.

Index

Note: the names, brief descriptions and website addresses of about seventy examples of people making significant contemporary contributions to the future of money are listed in Appendix 2, and not included in this Index.
